NEW
ENGLAND'S
SPECIAL
PLACES

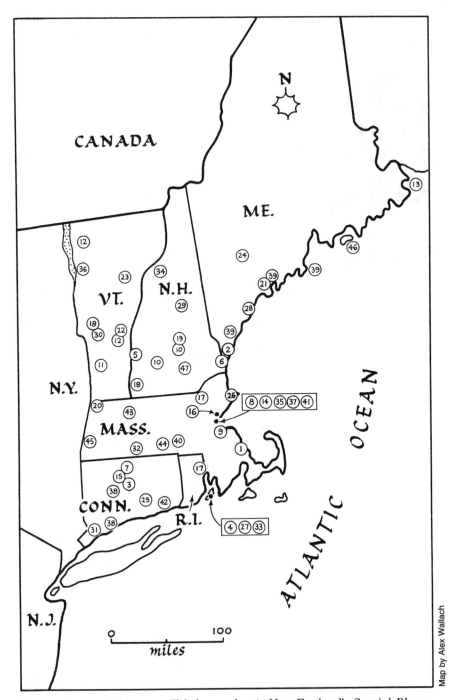

The numbers on this map will help you locate New England's Special Places. They correspond to the numbers that precede each place listed in the table of contents.

Map by Alex Wallach

NEW ENGLAND'S SPECIAL PLACES

Easy Outings to Historic Villages, Working Museums, Presidential Homes, Castles, and Other Year-Round Attractions

Michael A. Schuman

Revised, Expanded Edition

The Countryman Press, Woodstock, Vermont

To Patti, for her support.

© 1986, 1990 by Michael A. Schuman
All rights reserved
Second edition, third printing, 1993

Some of these articles appeared, in different form, in the *Keene Sentinel*, Keene, New Hampshire

Library of Congress Cataloging-in-Publication Data
Schuman, Michael.
   New England's special places : easy outings to historic villages,
working museums, presidential homes, castles, and other year-round
attractions / Michael A. Schuman. — 2nd ed.
      p.   cm.
   ISBN 0-88150-152-2
   1. New England—Description and travel—1981–   —Guide-books.
2. Historic sites—New England—Guide-books.   I. Title.
F2.3.S39   1989   89-25193
917.404'43—dc20   CIP

Designed by Leslie Fry
Frontispiece by Alex Wallach
Printed in the United States of America

CONTENTS

Introduction   7

COLONIAL NEW ENGLAND

(1) Plymouth, Massachusetts   11
(2) York Village, Maine   16
(3) Old Wethersfield, Connecticut   20
(4) Colonial Newport, Rhode Island   23
(5) Fort at No. 4; Charlestown, New Hampshire   28
(6) Strawbery Banke; Portsmouth, New Hampshire   31
(7) Old New-Gate Prison and Copper Mine; East Granby,
        Connecticut   34
(8) Bunker Hill; Boston, Massachusetts   38
    Additional Listings   42

THE OVAL OFFICE

(9) John and John Quincy Adams; Quincy, Massachusetts   45
(10) Franklin Pierce; Hillsboro and Concord, New Hampshire   49
(11) Robert Todd Lincoln; Manchester, Vermont   53
(12) Chester A. Arthur and Calvin Coolidge; Fairfield and
        Plymouth, Vermont   56
(13) Franklin D. Roosevelt; Campobello, New Brunswick   61
(14) John F. Kennedy; Boston, Massachusetts   65
(15) Museum of American Political Life; West Hartford,
        Connecticut   68
    Other Sites   72

WORKING IN NEW ENGLAND

(16) Saugus Iron Works National Historic Site; Saugus,
        Massachusetts   77
(17) Lowell National Historical Park and Slater Mill Historic
        Site; Pawtucket, Rhode Island, and Lowell,
        Massachusetts   80
(18) New England Maple Museum and sugarhouses; Pittsford,
        Vermont, and Monadnock Region of New Hampshire   85
(19) Shaker Village; Canterbury, New Hampshire   89
(20) Western Gateway Heritage State Park; North Adams,
        Massachusetts   93
(21) Maine Maritime Museum; Bath, Maine   97
(22) Billings Farm and Museum; Woodstock, Vermont   101

(23) Rock of Ages granite quarry; Barre, Vermont 105
(24) Norlands Living History Center; Livermore, Maine 108
Additional Listings 112

CASTLES AND MANSIONS

(25) Gillette Castle; East Haddam, Connecticut 117
(26) Hammond Castle; Gloucester, Massachusetts 121
(27) Beechwood; Newport, Rhode Island 124
(28) Victoria Mansion; Portland, Maine 128
(29) Castle in the Clouds; Moultonboro, New Hampshire 132
(30) Wilson Castle; Proctor, Vermont 135
(31) Lockwood-Mathews Mansion; Norwalk, Connecticut 138
Additional Listings 142

SPORTS AND LEISURE

(32) Naismith Memorial Basketball Hall of Fame; Springfield,
Massachusetts 145
(33) International Tennis Hall of Fame; Newport, Rhode Island 149
(34) New England Ski Museum; Franconia, New Hampshire 152
(35) New England Sports Museum; Boston, Massachusetts 155
(36) Shelburne Museum; Shelburne, Vermont 159
(37) Computer Museum; Boston, Massachusetts 163
(38) Barnum Museum and New England Carousel Museum;
Bridgeport and Bristol, Connecticut 167
(39) Maine Transportation (Boothbay Railway Village, Owls
Head Transportation Museum, Seashore Trolley
Museum); Boothbay, Owls Head, and Kennebunkport, Maine 171
Additional listings 176

OPEN ALL WINTER

(40) Higgins Armory Museum; Worcester, Massachusetts 179
(41) Charlestown Navy Yard (USS *Constitution*, Constitution
Museum, USS *Cassin Young*); Boston, Massachusetts 183
(42) Nautilus Submarine and Memorial Museum; Groton,
Connecticut 187
(43) Historic Deerfield; Deerfield, Massachusetts 191
(44) Old Sturbridge Village; Sturbridge, Massachusetts 194
(45) Norman Rockwell Museum at the Old Corner House;
Stockbridge, Massachusetts 197
(46) Off-Season in Acadia National Park; Bar Harbor, Maine 201
(47) Currier Gallery of Art; Manchester, New Hampshire 205
Additional Listings 208

INTRODUCTION

NOW THERE ARE EVEN MORE SPECIAL PLACES.

This second edition of *New England's Special Places* offers visits to many more attractions than the first edition. Some are newly opened, like Connecticut's Carousel Museum, or have undergone major facelifts, like the Barnum Museum in Bridgeport; both are featured in a light-hearted trip in the "Sports and Leisure" section.

Other new destinations are in regions of New England that were left untapped in our first edition, such as western Connecticut and mid-coastal Maine; it's in Maine that you will find a trio of museums devoted to antique transportation—narrow-gauge railways, trolleys, Model T's, and open cockpit airplanes.

In addition, we have updated the description of every attraction retained from the first edition. You would be surprised how many have changed significantly within a span of just a few years. Two special places featured in the first edition have permanently closed their doors. Several others have consolidated or expanded and little resemble their 1986 descriptions. Also revised are essential details such as hours, admission policies, and phone numbers; much of Massachusetts has a new telephone area code, and this is reflected in the second edition.

Of course, our basic criteria have not changed. Each place featured must offer insights into New England's character, whether it be the home of a president or the wilds of Acadia National Park in the off-season. Also important is geographical diversity, wider than ever in this expanded edition; from Fairfield County, Connecticut to Campobello Island, off the coast of easternmost Maine, we have New England well covered. Finally, we considered the quality of each attraction and are not including any place we would not recommend to a friend. Of course, some are better than others, but time spent in each destination is worth your while and can yield unexpected dividends.

Every attraction featured in this book was researched and visited by the author. While all details have been verified by press time, changes in operating procedures, hours or admission policies can always occur. If you are planning a special trip or are traveling a great distance, we recommend calling or writing in advance.

Whether you are seeing New England for the first time or have been exploring the region all your life, we are sure you will find that each place in this book reflects in its own way a part of New England's character.

Happy traveling, again!

M.A.S.

COLONIAL
NEW
ENGLAND

Streets that were dirt and cobbled are now paved with asphalt. Business as usual is conducted daily in harbors where gun boats bellowed with booms of cannons aimed at hilltop forts. On their way to school, children walk past split level homes with satellite dishes, past plots of land where rosemary was once grown to relieve pain from bruises, and near saltbox houses where people dipped candles to light their living quarters.

New Englanders today are still close to their colonial roots, sometimes closer than they realize. It doesn't matter if the first sight their ancestors saw as they arrived at America's shores was a rock on the Massachusetts coastline or a standing lady holding a torch in New York Harbor. Or even a single-span suspension bridge over the Golden Gate. If you live in New England, you reside in a place where colonists trod with muskets in hand at a time when a drink with the guys at the neighborhood bar meant a swig of flip at a patriot—or a Tory—tavern.

You can visit a vestige of colonial New England within a short drive from wherever you live in the six states. Most colonial attractions hug the shore, where the feet of settlers first met rocks and sand. In a region where states share cozy borders with one another and the coastline is extensive, you can find reproduced colonies, preserved neighborhoods or battlefields across parts of five states from York, Maine, to Groton, Connecticut.

But people don't stand still. Inevitably, they grow restless. And within a few years after the initial landings, western migration had started. Soon, there were settlements in the wide-open frontier of the Connecticut River Valley. Today, communities like Wethersfield and East Granby, Connecticut, and Charlestown, New Hampshire provide glimpses of life in colonial times; the settings are varied, since travelers can get a feel for early American living in a conserved village, an underground prison or a fortified palisade.

You need not be a history aficionado to enjoy visiting sights relating to our colonial past; you don't need to be able to recall the year the Boston Tea Party occurred or what positions, if any, were held by persons with names like John Alden or Roger Williams. You just need a bit of imagination, a sense of wonder, a desire to learn and a willingness to have a little fun.

PLYMOUTH, MASSACHUSETTS

It's just another day in 17th-century Plimoth Colony.

A WORD OF WARNING: WHEN TOURING PLIMOTH PLANTATION, THE RE-created Pilgrim village, don't ask the costumed residents about John Adams or Thomas Jefferson.

The only response you will get will be a look of bewilderment.

And while you're at it, stay away from questions about the American Revolution. You'll hear nothing short of verbal scorn as your answer.

You will, however, be able to get answers to most any question about the Pilgrims or Plymouth's early history at other historic sites such as Pilgrim Hall, the Sparrow House and Plymouth Rock.

Not that we are implying that the staff persons at Plimoth Plantation are unfriendly. It is just that they don't stop at simply interpreting life as it was in a Pilgrim village in 1627. They play the roles of actual settlers at the seven-year-old colony. Adams and Jefferson won't be born for 100 years and talk of revolution is ludicrous.

In fact, when one onlooker from the 20th century asked a villager who was feeding his pigs, "Do you think you will be a great nation some day?" the Pilgrim stopped his chores abruptly, turned to the inquisitive visitor and announced, "We are a great nation! We are England!"

The level of accuracy here, as you can tell by the nationalistic "Englishman," has been developed to include the people as well as the buildings and furnishings. Their English accents reflect the regions of the motherland that they called home. The primary attractions at Plimoth Plantation are really the people playing the parts and not simply the houses where they lived or their wooden implements.

Unlike other re-created villages, Plimoth Plantation's structures have all been built from scratch, as were the authentic-looking objects inside them. And unlike others, this is a reproduction of an actual place—New Plimoth colony in 1627.

The buildings, therefore, are relatively similar with subtle differences. Some have thatched roofs while others are shingled, for instance. But they all have dirt or plank floors and are spartan inside. The Pilgrim residents, whether famous like William Bradford or just one of the crowd, bring this place to life. You will leave here appreciating the 1980s!

Noticing the cramped quarters and the lack of amenities, one time-traveler from the 20th century asked, "Where do you bathe? In the ocean?"

"Immerse our bodies in water?" bellowed the shocked Pilgrim in disbelief. "That would wash off our protective oils. They are put on our bodies to protect us from pestilence."

Yes, you will appreciate modernity.

As you discuss the day's attitudes and ideas with the Pilgrims, don't be surprised if they ask you to hand them the roughhewn broom sitting in the corner or to pick up the wooden spoons or bowls. Plimoth Plantation is different from other such villages for another reason: it follows the "do touch" way of thinking, and visitors, especially young ones, are often encouraged to lend a hand patching a mud wall or drying some herbs.

If you arrive with an hour or so to spare, stop first at the *Mayflower II*. This accurate duplicate of the original 17th-century merchant vessel sailed here from Plymouth, England, in 1957, and over eight million 20th-century residents have walked its three decks since.

The time on the boat is February 1621, two months after it arrived from England and, as at the plantation, the settlers-to-be and the deckhands are able to answer questions only up to and including that time. Most of the settlers, you find out while on board, are ashore building the foundations of their village after spending months aboard this 106½-foot-long ship.

So most of the people you meet on the ship are the Pilgrims' wives and the crew, many of whom are looking forward to their return trip to England. We asked one woman working on an embroidery what she thought the future would bring. She declined to answer, fearing that should anyone overhear her predict the future, she might be accused of witchcraft. Better to ask questions about religious separatism, the voyage across the Atlantic, or the size of the ship's forecastle.

After leaving the 17th century behind, a good place to head is the Pilgrim Hall Museum, the repository for many of the Pilgrims' authentic possessions. And for other period pieces as well.

There's the *Sparrow-Hawk* as an example. It sits there stark, like the interior of some nautical dinosaur, looking much like a seagoing behemoth's exposed rib cage. But by today's standards, the ship *Sparrow-Hawk* was a lilliput. In fact, it was tiny even in relation to the *Mayflower*. Only 40 feet long, it is believed to have set sail from England in 1626 bound for Virginia. It ran aground near Chatham Bar on Cape Cod and was buried until a storm uncovered its timbers in 1863.

After being exhibited on Boston Common and other locations, it was placed in Pilgrim Hall in 1889 and has rested its weary planks here ever since.

You will see more than just the *Sparrow-Hawk*. There are some exhibits which you would expect to find here, Elder Brewster's stern, wooden chair as an example; while others may take you by surprise, like the rare 17th-century Pilgrim armor.

There is also John Alden's Bible, a wicker cradle that (legend has it) was used by the first baby born on the *Mayflower*, and the wool cloak with velvet trim that Governor Bradford's daughter was said to have worn for her wedding. But this array of artifacts is not just an unorganized hodgepodge; the displays are neatly organized by category.

Any first-time visitor will want to make the obligatory stop at Plymouth Rock, under its handsome portico that was designed by the famous architectural firm, McKim, Meade and White.

But this little glacial boulder comprised of Dedham granodiorite did not always sit under this attractive Grecian canopy. It was originally placed beneath a liberty pole in a main square in Plymouth shortly before the start of the American Revolution, only to be relocated to sundry other parts of Plymouth over the next century and a half; at one point, it was surrounded by a circular iron fence and placed in front of Pilgrim Hall, earning itself the tag, "The Rock in the Gilded Cage."

Plymouth Rock—the date, 1620, cut into it in 1880, etching in stone what had previously appeared in paint—was placed in its current location in 1921 as part of the tercentenary celebration commemorating the 300th anniversary of the Pilgrims' landing. The waterfront was re-landscaped so the rock could be placed at water level where the high tide would envelop it as it did when the Pilgrims first landed.

The oldest original house in Plymouth is the Richard Sparrow House at 42 Summer Street. Built in 1640, it today serves as both a museum and a craft shop. Resident potter Lois Atherton makes high quality porcelain and stoneware pottery in the home, and if you visit here after seeing Plimoth Plantation, you will likely have seen the approximately 100 pieces displayed there that she has created.

Atherton's demonstrations are catch-as-catch-can, but you can always purchase some of her handmade works like an English porcelain mug ($12), a reproduction oil lamp ($10), or a multi-handeled drinking vessel called a tyge ($24). Ironworks, weavings, baskets, and candles made by other Massachusetts craftspersons are also for sale.

Other than turkey, the food most persons associate with Thanksgiving is the cranberry. In fact, if the question should ever arise in Trivial Pursuit, let it be known that there are only three native American fruits: the blueberry, the Concord grape, and the cranberry. This, as well as the origin behind the naming of the cranberry and the difference between wet and dry harvesting are some of the other bits of lore you learn at Cranberry World Visitors Center. Though technically not a colonial attraction of Plymouth, this stop is included because the cranberry is so closely associated with this part of Massachusetts. You end your visit here with a sampling of different juices and a look at old Ocean Spray television commercials.

Other colonial Plymouth area sights? The list includes: First House and 1627 House, located by Plymouth Rock and owned and maintained by Plimoth Plantation. You should stop here if you don't have time to visit Plimoth Plantation. Howland House, a restored Pilgrim house dating from 1667. Harlow Old Fort House, dating from 1677 and featuring colonial crafts demonstrations. Coles Hill, where Pilgrims who died in the first winter were buried. Today it features a statue of Wampanoag Indian chief and friend to the Pilgrims, Massasoit, as well as a stellar view of Plymouth Harbor. And Burial Hill, where Governor Bradford is buried.

Location: Plymouth is 37 miles south of Boston. **Information:** Plymouth County Development Council, P.O. Box 1620, Pembroke, MA 02359; (617) 826-3136.

Location: Plimoth Plantation is on Route 3A (Warren Avenue), three miles south of downtown Plymouth. The *Mayflower II* is berthed on Water Street at the State Pier. The First House and 1627 House are on Water Street near the *Mayflower II*. **Admission** is charged to all attractions. A discounted combination ticket is available for Plimoth Plantation and the *Mayflower II*. **Hours:** All are open April through November, daily. **Allow** two to four hours at Plimoth Plantation and 30 minutes to an hour on the *Mayflower II*. **Information:** For all attractions, Plimoth Plantation, P.O. Box 1620, Plymouth, MA 02360; (508) 746-1622.

Location: Pilgrim Hall Museum, 75 Court Street. **Admission** is charged. **Hours:** Year-round, daily. Closed Christmas and New Year's Day. **Allow** one hour to one and a half hours. **Information:** (508) 746-1620.

Location: Richard Sparrow House, 42 Summer Street. **Admission** is charged. **Hours:** Memorial Day through Christmas Eve, daily except Wednesday. **Allow** a half hour. **Information:** (508) 747-1240.

Location: Cranberry World, 225 Water Street. **Admission** is free. **Hours:** May through November, daily. **Allow** a half hour. **Information:** (508) 747-2350.

Location: Howland House, 33 Sandwich Street. **Admission** is charged. **Hours:** July through mid-October, daily. **Information:** (508) 746-9590.

YORK VILLAGE, MAINE

What's on tap? A tour of Old York's Jefferds Tavern led by an interpreter in period costume.

Photo by Michael Schuman

O N ANY GIVEN DAY, YOU ARE LIKELY TO FIND A COOK OR OTHER PERSON garbed in 18th-century attire baking gingerbread in the Jefferds Tavern fireplace or explaining how the tavern owner kept track of his pints and quarts. The tavern is one of the six colonial buildings kept open to the public by the York Historical Society.

Each of this early American half-dozen presents a different view of colonial American life. There is the tavern, a schoolhouse, a jail, a residence that served numerous commercial purposes, a dockside warehouse, and a colonial revival home, all individual facets of what adds up to a jewel of a restored colonial village.

Here is a rundown on the Old York Historical Society's six museum buildings.

The Old Gaol: It was 2 P.M. but it could have been 2 A.M. I couldn't see the notepad that I held in my hand. I couldn't discern the features of the people standing next to me. And I couldn't fathom the thought of being forced to reside in this dark, dank jail cell.

The interpreter explained, "The natural light you see coming through the three small windows was all the light the prisoners had, other than from the wick of an occasional candle."

You can still see the 200-year-old bars on the windows as you proceed on your half-hour-long guided tour which points out other reminders of this building's inhospitable purpose: leg irons, handcuffs, rumpled straw mattresses, and numbers carved into the wooden floor, products perhaps of the idle hands of a homesick colonial prisoner anxious for release.

The three-and-one-half-foot thick original walls made of wood, iron, and granite exist, too. They separate the cells from the living quarters where the jail keeper and his family resided. You likely will be surprised to see the barred windows of one cell sharing a wall with the bedroom where the jail keeper's children slept. That's what we call confidence in security.

The Old Schoolhouse: Here is the archetypical old-fashioned school-house with its slates, wooden benches and quill pens.

Built in 1745, it is displayed as it would have appeared in colonial York. Exhibits afford a look at early New England education; the Lord's Prayer and The Ten Commandments were standard reading material in children's primers, and it was as early as 1782 that the first American speller was published by Noah Webster.

If you have restless children, consider buying a pamphlet here titled, "A Young Person's Guide to One Room Schoolhouses, 1700–1900" for 50 cents. It has quizzes, arithmetic questions and even a reprint of an early primer. Example: "How many inches from Exeter to Dover, it being 18 miles?" And it will keep the kids busy as you tour the old buildings.

Emerson-Wilcox House: Through the years, this house has served as a tavern, a tailor shop, a general store, a post office and a residence. Exhibits inside highlight the house's early purposes.

A stagecoach schedule, offering departure and arrival times for the "mail stage from Boston to Campden" hangs on the wall of the tap room, and a "tin kitchen" (rotisserie) rests by the fireplace as a reminder of the patrons served warm grub in this room. In the adjacent buttery are a tamarind jar and an olive jar, symbols of York's place as a seaport town. There are hops hanging near the fireplace, typical of a time when home brewing was a common practice.

The early post office represents the days when customers paid to receive, not send, their mail, and the elegant dining room is set for guests to arrive on Court Day when the visiting judges would come to York to hear cases. You can read a copy of a typical Court Day menu which rests on the dining room table; it includes: mackerel, roast turkey, chicken, stewed peas, mutton chops, fricassee of rabbit, apricot tart, and custards. Antacids were not included.

Upstairs, interpreter Barbara Grace showed us a set of antique fabrics which she labeled as "the only complete set of such 18th-century crewel hangings that we know of." And she wasn't just referring to York or even the state of Maine. Grace was talking about the entire United States.

Elizabeth Perkins House: The interpreter on duty in this house on the banks of the York River, explained, "We don't interpret the house as much as the person and the time."

The person was Elizabeth Perkins, who originally summered here from New York City. She travelled the world and "was blunt often to the point of tactlessness."

But she was also instrumental in preserving many of York's landmarks, including many opened to the public by the Old York Historical Society.

The time is the colonial revival period, which peaked around the turn of the 20th century. Although the earliest part of this house was built in the 18th century, the house is decorated according to the tastes of an eclectic collector 150 years later. It is authentic even to the point of including the inaccurate perceptions people of Perkins's era had of colonial New Englanders. For example, the beams are exposed, although the style in colonial New England was to cover them; Dutch colonial settlers in New York state were more inclined to leave beams exposed.

Jefferds Tavern: Originally a lively tavern in the nearby town of Wells, the building was moved to York in 1939. It is furnished to appear as it did when it served as a social center for area gentlemen who would eat, drink, smoke, stay warm by the fire on a frigid Maine winter night and discuss community affairs of the day.

Transients who stayed overnight rented only bed space, not entire rooms. Privacy was a low priority and it wasn't uncommon for guests not travelling together to sleep in one bed. In this tavern they likely would have stayed in the Jefferds family bedroom upstairs.

Before leaving the tavern, stop and take a look at the Federal period garden, which reflects one that would have existed around 1790. Flax, peas, beets, radishes, onions and squash are grown in raised beds and marigolds are planted to ward off pests.

John Hancock Warehouse and Wharf: Yes, John Hancock did own this warehouse, originally a customs house on the shores of the York River, but only for a period of five years. A friend who had owned it mortgaged it over to Hancock after experiencing financial difficulties.

The interpreter showed us a hypothetical cabin boy's trunk packed as if he was about to accompany a crew headed for the waters of the West Indies. Included in it are a pair of wool pants, a fife, a picture of his mother, a deck of cards, some hardtack and a Bible.

As you walk through the warehouse, you will detect the fragrant scents of tea, coffee, salt codfish, and other delicacies that one would have sensed 200 years ago. If you follow your eyes as well as your nose, you will head upstairs to the second floor which houses an ambitious display on life and industries on the York River.

Location: York is about 10 miles over the Maine border from New Hampshire. Four of the buildings comprising the Old York Historical Society are located on York Street (Route 1A) and Lindsay Road; the John Hancock Warehouse is on Lindsay Road by the York River and the Elizabeth Perkins House is across the York River on the right hand side after Sewall's Bridge. **Admission** is charged per building. A discounted combination ticket is available to all six buildings and is worthwhile if you plan on seeing more than two. **Hours:** Tuesday through Saturday, mid-June through September. **Allow** a half day to see all six buildings. Tours in each building range from a half hour to 45 minutes. There is no tour in the Old Schoolhouse but a guide is on hand to answer questions. **Information:** Old York Historical Society, Box 312, York, ME 03909; (207) 363-4974. **Note:** Buy tickets at the Jefferds Tavern at the corner of York Street (Route 1A) and Lindsay Road.

OLD WETHERSFIELD

Photo by Michael Schuman

A classic colonial springtime setting: flower blossoms; a proud, clapboard home, and a sky-piercing white steepled church. That's Old Wethersfield.

MOST NEW ENGLANDERS WHO LIVE OUTSIDE A 50-MILE RADIUS OF downtown Hartford have never heard of Old Wethersfield. And many who do live within that circle may be familiar with this colonial neighborhood but can't claim even one visit. These unfortunates are missing a lot, including some of Connecticut's oldest houses, an array of quality shopping possibilities, and a bedroom in which George Washington really did sleep.

Most of the 200) to 300-year-old homes you will see are still privately owned, but, fortunately, several are open to the public. The bedroom in which George Washington rested his weary bones can be found in the Webb House, one of Connecticut's most historic houses, where the general and Comte de Rochambeau met in 1781 to discuss plans for the Battle of Yorktown, which subsequently ended the Revolutionary War.

The Yorktown Conference has made this 10-room Georgian-Colonial house the most important attraction here. It joins two other houses—the Silas Deane House and the Isaac Stevens House—to form the Webb-Deane-Stevens Museum.

Needless to say, a favorite room in the Webb house is the bedchamber where Washington slept, still decorated with the red-wool flocked wallpaper that was hung especially for his visit. Another is the Conference Room, where an old map of the colonies and a quill pen sit on a maple gateleg table surrounded by antique chairs.

Joseph Webb was a wealthy man, and the lavish furnishings inside his home reflect his socioeconomic status. Silas Deane, Connecticut's first diplomat, was also a rich man, and his house, next door to Webb's, boasts eight elegant rooms and an eye-catching hand-carved mahogany staircase original to the house.

The Connecticut-Georgian style Isaac Stevens House, on the other hand, offers a look at the lifestyle of the average central Connecticut citizen of the late 18th century. Its interior is stocked with many original Stevens family possessions, and children particularly will be fascinated with the collection of old dolls and toys on the second floor.

One block away from the Webb-Deane-Stevens Museum, on the corner of Broad and Marsh streets, is the Buttolph-Williams House, one of the state's oldest. David Buttolph, a leather worker, built this four-room house at the turn of the 18th century. In its day, it was quite a substantial house.

Tours of the Buttolph-Williams House last 45 minutes, and guides discuss its history and the background of nearly every furnishing or artifact inside. This home has been redecorated in period style and most visitors—even those who will never be mistaken for James Beard—seem to like "Ye Greate Kitchin" the best. Woodenware, called "treenware" in its day, fills the shelves, while iron trammels, wooden churns and bowls grace the hearth and beehive oven.

While in the neighborhood, you might also take a look at the town meetinghouse, now the First Church of Christ. It is a white-steepled brick structure, completed in 1764. The Ancient Burial Ground behind the church has gravestones dating back to 1648.

You won't have to be in Wethersfield very long to hear about Comstock,

Ferre & Company, a seed business that has been in existence for more than 160 years. Today, you can buy seeds as well as perennials, herbs, flowers, fragrant soaps, potpourri, gourmet cooking wares, foods, and more at the ten-building complex at 263 Main. One building, the Old Onion House, dates back to the turn of the century, and at one time was used to provide winter-long storage for carloads of onion sets; it is now home to sweeter smelling flowers.

Those interested in hand-crafted articles might want to inspect the offerings at Charlie and Barbara Ford's House of Images at 147 Main Street; prints, candles and stained glass are some of the items for sale. Christmas shops are obligatory nowadays in tourist centers, and Wethersfield is no exception. The Red Barn Christmas Shop, which opens for the season in August, shares 133 Main with the Enchanted Heart (gifts and imports).

There's a trio of shoppers' lures at 217 Main: Ruth Bauer's Olde Towne Doll Shop, Infinity's Curiosity Shop (antiques and collectibles) and Sweet Gatherings, an old-time ice cream parlor. Other nearby stores are The Mulberry Tree at 233 Main (boutiques and gifts), Jewelry by Neill Walsh at 285 Main and The Depot Stock Exchange Antiques at 212 Church Street.

Location: Old Wethersfield is south of Hartford. To reach Old Wethersfield, take Interstate 91 south to exit 26 and follow the signs from the exit. **Admission** is charged to the Webb-Deane-Stevens Museum. **Admission** is charged to the Buttolph-Williams House and is free to the First Church of Christ. **Hours:** The Webb-Deane-Stevens Museum is open year-round. The Buttolph-Williams House is open mid-May to mid-October. The Webb-Deane-Stevens Museum is open Tuesday through Sunday (afternoon only on Sunday) and the Buttolph-Williams House is open daily, afternoons only. The First Church of Christ is open by chance or by appointment. Most stores are open year round, Tuesday through Saturday. **Allow** ninety minutes to see the complete Webb-Deane-Stevens Museum and 30 minutes to see the Buttolph-Williams House. **Information:** Wethersfield Historical Society, 150 Main Street, Wethersfield, CT 06109; (203) 529-7656. Webb-Deane-Stevens Museum, (203) 529-0612. Buttolph-Williams House, (203) 529-0460. First Church of Christ, (203) 529-1575. **Note:** Picnic tables are available for use at Wethersfield Cove at the north end of Main Street.

NEWPORT

Photo by Michael Schuman

The columns on the right represent the tribes of ancient Israel and the candelabra in the Touro Synagogue dates to the 1760s.

THE HISTORY OF NEWPORT, RHODE ISLAND, DOES NOT START WITH the Gilded Age. In colonial times, this small city was a center of seaside commerce and social activity on a par with Boston, New York, Philadelphia, and Charleston, South Carolina.

Long before it was regarded as a playground for America's millionaires, Newport, and all of Rhode Island, became known as a haven for those seeking religious liberty. The state's founder, Roger Williams, had been banished from Puritan Massachusetts Bay Colony and, as a result, planned for The State of Rhode Island and Providence Plantations (the state's official title) to be a place where the government would have no power over spiritual matters.

Ironically, while Newport offered religious freedom to so many, it was also a pivotal point in the African slave trade in the early 18th century, with as many as 60 ships dealing in slaves as well as in other commodities like foodstuffs and sperm whale oil, which was made into candles.

Later on, Newport became a hotbed literally and figuratively during the American Revolution. Newporters set fire to one British ship and attacked several others before being occupied by British forces for two years. It was only after France entered the war that Newport was liberated.

Although the mansions of the Vanderbilts, the Astors, the Oelrichses and the rest might be top priorities on visitors' agendas today, one can still investigate the colonial history of this town on Aquidneck Island by visiting its landmark buildings. We will take a close look at three, each of which illustrates a different aspect of Newport's early days: freedom given to religious minorities, the late colonial period and the early colonial period.

Touro Synagogue National Historic Site: Because of the rare religious freedom and absence of persecution found here, Newport became a haven for Sephardic Jews, those whose family roots were in Spain and Portugal. Many, called Marranos, converted to Christianity to avoid persecution. Others had been driven from their homelands and lived in other parts of Europe, South America or the West Indies.

Although Jews had lived in Newport for more than a century, Newport's first synagogue wasn't dedicated until 1763. It was called Congregation Yeshuat Israel (The Salvation of Israel) but later became known as the Touro Synagogue. Why did the less formal name take over? Nobody knows for sure. Some believe it was named for its first cantor, Reverend Isaac Touro. Synagogue historian Bernard Kusinitz, however, thinks the name change came much later in 1883 when it was rededicated; Kusinitz states that it is more likely that it was named for the street on which it was located, Touro Street, as was the custom of English and American congregations.

The building still stands, making it the oldest synagogue in the United States. But as important as Touro Synagogue National Historic Site is for its symbolic tribute to the separation of church and state and the principles of religious liberty, it is also an architectural masterpiece designed by one of mid-18th-century America's most respected colonial architects, Peter Harrison.

Harrison adapted the synagogue to the styles of his time by applying the principles of Georgian architecture. It was planned that the building would sit in a diagonal position so the congregation when standing before the Holy Ark would face eastward towards Jerusalem. The free 15-minute tour emphasizes the colonial era furnishings, some of which are original. The Windsor chairs and settees, however, are reproductions; in fact, at the time of the synagogue's dedication, there were no chairs in the main hall and men could sit only on a wainscoted bench along the walls. As in all Orthodox synagogues, women sat upstairs in the gallery and men sat downstairs.

An original deerskin Torah sits in a protective glass-enclosed case next to the Holy Ark. A representation of the Ten Commandments, painted by Newport artist Benjamin Howland, sits above the Ark while 12 Ionic columns support the gallery and 12 Corinthian columns support the domed ceiling; each set of columns represents the 12 Tribes of Israel.

In the early 19th century, the Sephardic community in Newport dispersed and from the 1820s until 1883, the synagogue fell out of use. Today, however, it is the home of a congregation consisting of nearly 145 families entirely of Ashkenazi (northern and eastern European) backgrounds. One thing hasn't changed: the congregation, like the original one more than 200 years ago, adheres to Orthodox traditions.

Hunter House: A couple of decades before the founding of the synagogue, Jonathan Nichols, Jr., was building a home that still stands. It became recognized during his lifetime as "the mansion of hospitality."

But it wouldn't become known by his name. Nor by that of the next owner. After Nichols's death, Joseph Wanton, Jr., bought the house and owned it until he died in 1780. The American revolution devastated Newport, and the house at 54 Washington Street, like the rest of the city, suffered through decades of neglect. It was not until 1805 when lawyer, politician and Newport native William Hunter bought the house that it would again have long-term owners. Long-term they were; the Hunter family resided in the house for nearly five decades.

And so the structure was to become known as the Hunter House. It was the first building bought by The Preservation Society of Newport County, and is the only colonial era house which they maintain. (The society operates many of the famous Newport mansions.) It is regarded as one of Rhode Island's most beautiful homes of the period and it is a showcase for furniture made by Townsend and Goddard of Newport.

The cabinet of a Hepplewhite tall clock downstairs is a Townsend and Goddard product. A small upstairs bedroom boasts four Townsend and Goddard chairs, and a mahogany card table with maple inlay rests in the gentlemen's sitting room and was constructed by these two Newport natives.

How can you tell Townsend and Goddard works? They left their signatures in special ways, said our guide, pointing out the fluted legs, clawed legs and slippered feet on some of the chairs and tables.

The twisted design of its hand-carved balusters has made the mahogany staircase one of the home's more memorable features, although many visitors are attracted to the pine paneling; in some cases, as many as 14 layers of paint had to be removed in order to expose the original wood.

The carved wooden pineapple over the front door symbolizes the home's less formal name, "the mansion of hospitality," although our guide told us that there were times when the owners may not have appeared to be full of warm welcomes. In earlier times, guests ushered into the tea room were served only a half cup of tea. If they had the audacity to ask for more, they were given a firm "no," and in many cases were never invited back. Tea was just too expensive, even in "the mansion of hospitality."

Wanton-Lyman-Hazard House: This home, tucked in among the buildings on Broadway, predates the Hunter House by nearly half a century and is a superb example of First Period architecture. It is now owned and operated by the Newport Historical Society.

Built before 1700, the house had a succession of owners, including Colonial Governor Richard Ward and an unpopular Tory named Martin Howard, who was burned in effigy during the 1765 Newport riots against the hated Stamp Act. As violence escalated, mobs attacked the home and reportedly smashed doors and broke Howard's furniture. Our guide told us that the rioters also looped a rope around the chimney and tried in vain to yank it down.

Subsequent owners after Howard gave the house its name. There was John G. Wanton, a Quaker merchant who, Newport deeds show, bought the house on September 23, 1765, and who paid only 60 pounds to repair the damage done during the riots. (This price tag makes some believe that the extent of the vandalism was exaggerated.) Then there were Daniel Lyman, a colonial army major who married the Wantons' daughter; and Benjamin Hazard, a lawyer who married the Lymans' daughter.

You can pick out the early floorboards when you tour the house; just look for those with knots in them. Most of the colonial furniture is authentic to the period, though not necessarily the house. The keeping room, where many of the children would have slept, is the epitome of the colonial bedroom, where you will find a rope bed with a trundle bed hidden underneath. Our guide showed us a wooden implement used to tighten the ropes of the bed, and we learned that through this practice, the expression, "Sleep tight" came into being.

One of the oddest curiosities in this storied home is the tiny invalid's chair, also called a grandmother's chair. Dating from the mid 18th-century, the chair has a canted back and when in use, leaned flush against the wall. Yet it was highly portable, and could easily be carried up and down stairs, even when occupied by an elderly person or a sickly child.

Location: Newport is 35 miles south of Providence. **Information:** Newport Chamber of Commerce, 10 America's Cup Avenue, Newport, RI 02840, (401) 847-1600.

Location: Touro Synagogue National Historic Site, 85 Touro Street. **Admission** is free. **Hours:** Mid-June through Labor Day, Sunday through Friday; afternoons in early spring and early autumn; Sunday afternoon the rest of the year. **Allow** 15 minutes to a half hour. **Information:** (401) 847-4794.

Location: Hunter House, 54 Washington Street. **Admission** is charged. A discounted combination ticket including admission to Hunter House and all sites operated by The Preservation Society of Newport County (many of the famous mansions and Green Animals topiary in nearby Portsmouth, Rhode Island) is available. **Hours:** May through September, daily; April and October weekends. **Allow** 45 minutes. **Information:** (401) 847-1000.

Location: Wanton-Lyman-Hazard House, 17 Broadway. **Admission** is charged. **Hours:** Summer season, Thursday through Sunday. **Allow** a half hour. **Information:** Newport Historical Society, 82 Touro Street, Newport, RI 02840, (401) 846-0813.

FORT AT NO. 4

Fort at No. 4's musket men explain the fine arts of colonial soldiery.

AT THE URGING OF PEOPLE DRESSED IN COLONIAL NEW ENGLAND'S latest fashions, I imagined that I was standing in the midst of the last outpost of civilization for hundreds of miles. Call me Ethan.

Said Louise Miller, a Fort-at-No. 4 administrator, "This was a new settlement in New England's frontier in 1746."

The costumed interpreters at the Charlestown, New Hampshire site convinced us to ignore all the boxy homes and modern, sleek cars. This was 1746. The fort was at the edge of the wilderness, and all that existed of Charlestown was inside it.

"The nearest, largest settlement to the south was Fort Dummer, near present-day Brattleboro. To the north and west was wilderness until you met the French settlements on Lake Champlain and at Montreal," explained Jeff Miller, another administrator who doubles as the fort's resident blacksmith.

Two musket men had just finished a firing demonstration when we entered the stockade on a muggy summer Sunday. Despite the steamy conditions, attention to accuracy was not compromised—Jeff Miller works in the blacksmith shop clad in a linen shirt despite the weather. He explained that in the mid-18th century an Englishman would never have removed his shirt. Knee-breeches of linen, wool, cotton, and sometimes leather, were the common attire for men. Research shows that trousers were not as prevalent then as today.

At this point in American history, clothing was made from purchased cloth or home-produced cloth. Settlers here traded with Captain Phineas Stevens who brought a very wide selection of cloth up from Northfield and Deerfield, Massachusetts. In his home at the fort, we saw bolts of cloth ready to be traded.

To see how such 18th-century attire was made, you can step inside Lt. Moses Willard's quarters where you will see an 18th century loom and an antique spinning wheel used for the home production of cloth. The final products of the craftspersons' efforts are not only displayed but are for sale in the gift shop as well.

Today the Obadiah Sartwell House is the center of the fort's culinary activity. You never know what the colonial cook might be putting together. On our visit, light, spicy cookies had just been baked in the house's brick oven.

Twentieth-century laws prevent taste-testing 18th-century goodies, but you can ask questions and learn just what kind of spices were used in that pumpkin pie, how long it took to make this loaf of bread, and just how much tedious labor is involved in maintaining and cleaning a beehive oven.

Don't hold back your inquiries regarding the utensils and furnishings you see. We noticed something that resembled a modern ice cube tray; only after asking did we hear that it was a colonial gem tin.

When we stepped into the Captain Phineas Stevens House, staff member Beatrice Olden took pleasure in describing to us the names and the uses of many antiquated oddities inside.

"The broom you see in this corner was actually made from this," she remarked, directing us toward a stack of broom corn looking much more like freshly harvested wheat. Moving to another part of the Stevens House, she introduced us to a bundle of other household items; a betty lamp, a hog scraper (which really did have the purpose of scraping hogs, at least part of the time), and a bulky yoke, used not by oxen but by people.

In the rear of the open one-room house are the sleeping quarters; in showing us the wide rope bed and the accompanying trundle bed for children, Olden indicated how a large colonial family could actually sleep in relative comfort.

When she is not showing visitors state-of-the-art 1746 kitchenware and bedroom furniture, Olden has the job of making candles the colonial way. As you watch her place them in a mold, you might hear that a family of four working from dawn to dusk could have made as many as 200 candles.

"But," she informed us, "they burned rather quickly and it took 24 hours for one mold of candles to harden."

Yet the crude mold she held was actually a luxury in the time portrayed here, and most families simply could not afford them. In addition, she related that fat rather than wax was the principal ingredient in candles on the American wilderness in 1746.

Location: Fort at No. 4 is on Route 11, one mile north of Charlestown, New Hampshire, and about nine miles south of Claremont, New Hampshire. From Interstate 91, take exit 7 (Springfield, Vermont-Charlestown exit); from Route 12, follow the signs in Charlestown. **Admission** is charged. **Hours:** Traditional Memorial Day through Columbus Day weekend, daily. **Allow** one to two hours. **Information:** Fort at No. 4, Box 336, Charlestown, NH 03603; (603) 826-5700.

STRAWBERY BANKE

Strawbery Banke: a centerpiece for colonial commerce where a famous author and a bad boy both grew up.

WILD STRAWBERRIES WERE GROWING IN PROFUSION ALONG THE PIScataqua River when Captain Walter Neal and his crew were sailing it and looking for a place to settle. The year was 1630 and Neal and his men had been sent to the New World by the Laconia Company, a group of London merchants. Unlike most of the other people coming to live on the newly discovered shores, they came to look not for religious freedom but for economic growth. But their noteworthiness stemmed from their name for this new land: Strawbery Banke.

The strawberries survived much longer than the business, which went bankrupt after only eight years. After a feeble attempt at self-government, the residents of Strawbery Banke gladly became part of the Massachusetts Bay Company in 1641; within a dozen years, residents of the settlement wanted to change its name.

"We are at the river's mouth and our port is as good as any in the land," said the settlers when petitioning the Massachusetts General

Court. The wish was granted and the new name for the community became Portsmouth.

Like many other original settlements in northern America's cities and towns, the riverside section of Portsmouth thrived as a seaport in the 18th century, became a bit heavy towards the industrial side in the 19th century, suffered from urban blight early in the 20th and was rescued by preservationists some decades later.

We heard Strawbery Banke's story, which we have summarized in a nutshell, as we strolled along the current Strawbery Banke's Jefferson Street, about as wide as a Honda Civic and nothing but dirt and gravel. We were on the Neighborhood Tour, given twice daily to acquaint visitors with the centuries of history to be found here.

Officials at Strawbery Banke, said while identifying houses along this glorified path called Jefferson Street, "This is not a recreated village. It's a preserved neighborhood. Strawbery Banke is a place with a long history and we show little bits and pieces of it. It's not like Old Sturbridge Village or Colonial Williamsburg where all has been reconstructed to show one period."

We continued walking, reaching a stopping point at the narrow intersection of Jefferson and Atkinson streets where our guide talked of colonial times. "It was very crowded here and very busy, filled with houses and stores." And we pictured paunchy wig-topped businessmen conducting business in the streets while deckhands and hearty sailors unleashed cargo at the port's edge.

Our guide led us across the street and we sat in the shady portion of a vacant lot. Behind us was an herb garden. A slaughterhouse originally stood there. And we were sitting where there once had been stables.

We got up and approached the courtyard of the Thomas Bailey Aldrich House, one of five completely furnished in period. It was a landmark long before Strawbery Banke opened to the public in 1965. As the birthplace and boyhood home of the famous author and editor, Thomas Bailey Aldrich—whose most famous work, *The Story of a Bad Boy*, was set in this house—this was a well recognized home in his lifetime, and after his death in 1907, it was preserved and opened to visitors as a memorial. It was operated over the next 71 years by the Thomas Bailey Aldrich Memorial Association until it became part of Strawbery Banke in 1979.

The Neighborhood Tour ended in this courtyard leaving us with a story about Aldrich and his friend, Mark Twain. The two authors had met outside of a bookstore when Aldrich told the author of *Tom Sawyer* and *Huckleberry Finn* that his books were no longer popular among American readers. When Twain questioned Aldrich's comment, the Portsmouth native invited Twain to step inside the bookstore. They saw a shelf full of Twain's books but none of Aldrich's.

"You see," said Aldrich with a smile, "you are not selling. They have sold out of mine."

But Aldrich was just being modest. He was highly successful and he broke traditional standards with *The Story of a Bad Boy;* it was the first children's story about a boy whose actions were bad but whose heart was good.

The story will mean more to you after you have stepped inside Aldrich's house, which has been restored to look as Aldrich described it in the book. The time is the 1850s and you can see the walls "covered with pictured paper representing landscapes and sea views" and the "large rooms wainscoted and rich in wood carvings about the mantelpieces."

Prior to its opening to the public, the Aldrich home served both as a hospital and a home for children, said our guide, typical of the staff persons on duty in each home. They will tell you as much or as little as you want to hear at each furnished house so you don't feel pressured and can either browse about at your own pace or ask questions about the furniture, art or bric-a-brac on view.

One visitor's curiosity was piqued when he saw sand on the kitchen floor in the colonial Wheelwright House. The interpreter explained that this was a common touch during that period and, surprisingly, not just for houses found along the coastline. Sand was put on the floor to absorb grease, commented our guide, who added that many historical diaries mention as much as three inches of grease collecting on the floor. And sand served other purposes, acting as an abrasive to help keep clean the pine floors in houses like this one. When the sand got too dirty, it was simply swept away and replaced with fresh sand.

Craftspersons are on hand in some homes here, such as the former Dinsmore Blacksmith Shop, today the residence of a cooper. At one time or another, you may also find a potter, weaver, cabinet maker and a wooden boat builder at work on the grounds.

Location: Strawbery Banke is located at Hancock and Marcy Streets, Portsmouth. From Interstate 95, take exit 7 (Market Street) and follow the signs. **Admission** is charged. **Hours:** May through October, daily. **Allow** two to four hours. **Information:** Strawbery Banke, P.O. Box 300, Portsmouth, NH 03801; (603) 433-1100. **Note:** Picnic tables are available for use in back of the Conant Coffee shop. You also can bring your own food with you and picnic on the grounds. Nice gift shops.

OLD NEW-GATE PRISON AND COPPER MINE

People once risked life to escape New-Gate Prison. Now they pay to get in.

THINK BACK TO ANY VACATION YOU HAVE TAKEN WHERE YOUR ITIN-
erary included a sightseeing venture in a famous cave. Mammoth Cave
National Park in Kentucky perhaps. Or Carlsbad Caverns National Park
in New Mexico. Or maybe New York's Howe Caverns.

Try to recall the chilly damp air, the clammy feeling. And the eery
darkness that engulfed you when the guide turned out the artificial lights.

If you had been found guilty of a crime in Connecticut in the early
years of our country's history, a similar cave would have been your home.

Your crime could have been as simple as adultery or as grave as murder.
Your sentence could have ranged anywhere from nine months to life.

But your home away from home would likely have been New-Gate
Prison in Simsbury, which on today's map is part of East Granby.

The underground hold that was to serve as a prison first gained fame
in colonial New England when copper was discovered here in 1707. For

almost seven decades thereafter, this area, which came to be known as "Copper Hill," was actively mined, and it is believed to be the first operating copper mine in the colonies.

At the outset, the mine was in the possession of local landowners. But ownership then passed through a slew of individuals, one of whom, Jonathan Belcher, would become governor of Massachusetts. And despite the initial enthusiasm of the owners, factors like the cost of shipping ore to England for smelting, the numerous shipwrecks of vessels transporting ore overseas and the lack of present day mining operations caused work to be stopped in 1773.

As you climb down the stairway that brings you into the mine, take a look at the left wall of the tunnel and you will still see veins of copper. New-Gate Guide Edwin Reinhold says the value is about 11 percent copper, although it has been reported that in some cases the value had been claimed as high as 50 percent.

"Glad I'm just visiting," sighed a middle-aged woman as she was finishing her underground stroll in the nippy 54-degree air. Her shivering from the cold prompted a question from her travelling companion. Noting that prisoners slept, ate, and worked here, she puzzled in a half-joking manner, "How many prisoners died from pneumonia?"

To which Guide Reinhold responded, "Surprisingly not many. One prisoner who kept a journal wrote, 'It was a very healthy place.' There is less bacteria at 50 degrees than there is at 70 degrees and the prisoners wore heavy homespun woolen clothing."

Reinhold then offered the suggestion, with sort of a take-it-or-leave-it attitude, that there may be some healing benefits from copper.

"There are people who believe in wearing copper bracelets, you know," Reinhold offered.

Whatever the reasons, the records show that the mortality rate was miniscule. In the period from 1790 to 1820, a total of 250 prisoners were kept here and only nine deaths were recorded.

The encouraging mortality statistics would have been of little solace to those interned here. Nearby in the dank cavern is the solitary confinement section where troublesome inmates were chained to the rock floor. You can still see where one guilty party hollowed out a hole in the floor, most likely to collect seepage to use as a drinking supply.

Not all of the prison was underground. In fact, the ruins of the prison walls introduce passersby on adjacent Newgate Road to the colonial prison. The sandstone walls formed the second barrier used to keep the prison residents inside. The first barricade was a picket fence with iron spikes on top, and was found to be ineffective. Similarly, brick walls were deemed obsolete as soon as they were built, since inmates had no trouble chipping away the mortar holding them together. You will notice a single chimney standing among the ruins at the rear of the prison yard. The bottom portion is made of sandstone while higher up, out of the reach of human arms, it is constructed of brick.

Keep an eye out as you walk about the grounds for the remaining bars used to restrain prisoners. There is one with a partial slice in it, a humble effort of one inmate who tried and failed in an escape attempt. Rumor has it that his weapon was a watch spring, and although nobody knows for certain, Reinhold recalled that a jeweler who toured the prison said it seemed a reasonable theory to him.

You will discover as you tour the prison yard and read the posted commentaries and descriptions that this was hardly a colonial Alcatraz. There were numerous successful escapes, including that of John Hinson, the prison's first inmate, who escaped after only 18 days in confinement. And an introductory tape explains, "He hasn't been seen since."

A copy of a posted prison notice issued at the time of Hinson's escape reads, "Last night escaped from New Gate Prison at Simsbury one John Hinson lately committed for Burglary who is about five feet six inches high, has black Eyes, dark Hair, of a fair Complexion and about twenty Years of Age—(he was helped out by some evil minded Persons from without)."

In addition to solitary confinement, there were other disciplinary actions meted out for those caught escaping or deemed incorrigible. Markers throughout the grounds denote the places where tools of punishment stood.

There was a whipping post, but the New-Gate administration, being rather progressive in its day, permitted only ten lashes. The prison keeper could place fetters and shackles on inmates, assign them to the dreaded treadmill duty, or reduce their daily food rations (which surprisingly were fairly ample—a typical daily ration included a pound of beef, a pound of bread, two pounds of potatoes, three and a half pints of cider and half a gill of rum for good behavior).

Some compassion was shown to those too ill to be kept in the cold and clammy caves. They were kept above ground in cells directly below the guardhouse and were admitted to their chambers through the use of trap doors. The maze of cells is still around; try to imagine the isolation while walking through them.

As you wander through the guard house, be sure to examine the old wanted posters ("STOP VILLAINS," one screams out) and the inventory of prisoners here on December 21, 1811, and their crimes. One prisoner named Clark Payne was given a steeper sentence for adultery (four years) than was another, named Charles Gilbert, for forgery (three years). Another prisoner arrested for forgery was slapped on the wrist with an 18-month sentence. And amazingly, a man in for bigamy was sentenced to only five months. (We imagine proper citizens must have been saying, "You bring the vermin in and the judges let them back on the street right away.")

Many, including women, were sentenced to life for more heinous crimes. One, Tera Mansfield, was in for murder. Others given life terms had been convicted of murder, attempt to poison, attempt to rape. Horse stealing couldn't have been a serious crime; a man convicted of it was given only a two-year term.

Also in the guardhouse are murals created for the bicentennial depicting New-Gate prison scenes. One shows criminals in 1827 being transferred from New-Gate to a new prison in Wethersfield, Connecticut. If you examine the faces, you might be a bit surprised. Artist David R. Wagner painted the faces of members of the state Historic Commission on the characters in the mural. The most recognizable is late Connecticut Governor Ella Grasso.

Location: Old New-Gate Prison and Copper Mine is at 115 Newgate Road, East Granby, Connecticut. From Interstate 91, take exit 40 (Route 20, Bradley International Airport). Follow Route 20 west for about six miles; take a right onto Newgate Road and follow the signs. **Admission** is charged. **Hours:** Mid-May through October, Wednesday through Sunday. **Allow** 45 minutes to an hour and a half. **Information:** Connecticut Historical Commission, 59 South Prospect Street, Hartford, CT 06106, (203) 653-3563 in season; (203) 566-3005 the rest of the year.

BUNKER HILL AND "WHITES OF THEIR EYES"

Courtesy: Boston National Historical Park

Bunker Hill Monument and USS Constitution.

Why would americans build a monument to a battle we lost? And why would we still remember it—in fact, make it a household word— more than two centuries later?

In the case of the Battle of Bunker Hill, there are good reasons. You can explore the history of the famed battle by visiting two sites in the Charlestown section of Boston.

Many historians compare the Battle of Bunker Hill, which actually was fought on Breed's Hill, to the first Battle of Bull Run in the Civil War. In both battles, the initial results were dwarfed by the overall importance in terms of the rebels' outlook.

It was June 17, 1775. Nearly two months earlier, the first shots had been fired at the skirmishes in Concord and Lexington. General Thomas Gage, royal governor and commander of the British Forces, had been planning to occupy the heights surrounding Boston. Bunker Hill, the highest point in Charlestown, afforded a commanding position over the harbor.

But on the morning of June 17, Gage and his men awoke to a surprise. The colonists were building fortifications on Breed's Hill, slightly lower than Bunker Hill but nearer the shore.

Although they could have cut off the American works from the rear, the British attacked from the front, expecting an American response of inaccurate musket fire, panic and retreat. They were in for a shock.

"Don't fire until you see the whites of their eyes," bellowed General Israel Putnam of the colonies (according to legend). "Fire low. Everyone of you can kill a squirrel at a hundred yards . . . pick off the commanders."

With their five-foot-long Brown Bess muskets, which shot bone- splitting one-ounce musket balls, the colonists aimed low. The British retreated and General John Stark, who had 1,200 New Hampshire troops in front of his barricade beside the Mystic River, said of the dozens of British dead, "I never saw sheep lie as thick in the fold."

The British retreated, regrouped and rallied, and again faced a dev- astating fire which forced them to retreat. It was said that in Jaffrey, New Hampshire, 75 miles away, workmen raising a new meeting house could hear the murderous fire.

At the shore, the British ships at anchor fired incendiary shells into the frame buildings of Charlestown and burned the town in a prelude to the third and final charge. The forces of Generals William Howe and Robert Pigot joined with those of Henry Clinton in this third assault. The colonists' ammunition and reinforcements ordered from Cambridge had not arrived. They halted the British advance until their ammunition was gone; as a last resort, they threw rocks and whatever other debris they could find. But finally, the Yankees were forced to retreat, with

Colonel Stark and his New Hampshire regiment holding out until the end.

So the British won the battle, but with grave consequences. About 475 of the 2,000 British were killed or later died of wounds received in the battle, while nearly 800 were wounded but survived. The American side had 140 killed, 271 wounded and 30 captured. General Howe later wrote, "When I look at the consequences, I do it with horror," and General Clinton said that another similar victory would ruin the British.

But the biggest casualty in the battle was the notion of American vulnerability and cowardice. The colonists had proven to themselves and to the British that they could take on the best organized troops. Never again in the war did the British attempt a frontal attack on American fortifications.

As with any confrontation, each side had its own story to tell. This is pointed out clearly in the multi-media presentation called "Whites of Their Eyes," which plays daily in the Bunker Hill Pavilion near the Charlestown Navy Yard.

With more than 1,000 color slides, 14 screens, 22 life-sized mannequins, and seven channels of sound, you are thrust into the middle of the action on and around Breed's Hill. There are sounds of musket fire and cannons, shouts and commands; thunderous booming is accompanied by flashes of light in a realistic special-effects array.

In addition to hearing the re-creation of the battle, you listen to both the British and colonists' points of view in the forms of two servicemen reading aloud letters they are writing home.

And while you leave with an understanding of the battle itself, you may also find yourself wondering about other battles and other wars in our history. The British strategy of formal fighting did little good in a strange land where the natives knew too well the peculiarities of the terrain, but it has been repeated in numerous situations throughout the last 200 years and as recently as the late 20th century. Comparisons to our role in Vietnam are inevitable.

From the Bunker Hill Pavilion, it's a walk of five to ten minutes to the 220-foot-high Bunker Hill Monument on Breed's Hill, the actual site of the battle. Construction on the monolith was started in 1826 and finished in 1842; it was built with nothing more than the strength of workers and the power of oxen and horses.

The cornerstone was laid in place in 1825 when the Marquis de Lafayette—the same Lafayette who had fought beside the colonists in the Revolutionary War—attended a ceremony to mark the battle's 50th anniversary. Massachusetts Congressman Daniel Webster, president of the Bunker Hill Monument Association, offered a speech in which he said that the monument would commemorate "the first great battle of the revolution and not only the first blow, but the blow that determined the conflict." Seventeen years later, Webster, then secretary of state of the United States, was on hand at the dedication.

At the base of the monument is a small museum, the highlight of which is an extensive diorama showcasing the battle site. A park ranger is on hand to offer periodic talks of 15 or 20 minutes. You can also climb the 294 steps to the top for a stellar view of Boston and its surroundings. There is no elevator, and, regardless of the shape you believe you are in, you might be dismayed to realize that you have to pause now and then on the way up or that your legs feel as if they are filled with jelly after the walk down.

Location: It is best to park near the Bunker Hill Pavilion at the parking lot for Charlestown Navy Yard visitors. From Interstate 93, take Route 1; then take the immediate exit (Constitution Road). The Bunker Hill Monument is a ten-minute walk from the parking lot.

"Whites of Their Eyes." **Admission** is charged. **Hours:** year-round, daily; closed Thanksgiving, Christmas, New Year's Day. **Allow** a half hour. **Information:** (617) 241-7575.

Bunker Hill Monument. **Admission** is free. **Hours:** Year-round, daily; closed Christmas. **Allow** an hour to climb the monument and see the museum, more to hear the talk by a park ranger. **Information:** Boston National Historical Park, 15 State Street, Boston, MA 02109; (617) 242-5691.

Note: Boston National Historical Park contains many more of the Hub's best known historical sites. The list includes: the Old State House, Paul Revere's House, the Old South Meeting House, the memorial tower and greensward at Dorchester Heights, Faneuil Hall, the Old North Church, and the USS Constitution (see "Open All Winter" section).

ADDITIONAL LISTINGS

Here is a list of other historic sights in New England which interpret some aspects of colonial living. Although there are some attractions which are discussed in other chapters that also reflect colonial New England life, we are limiting this list only to those places not mentioned elsewhere in the book.

Coventry, CT. Nathan Hale Homestead. Mid-May through mid-October. (203) 742-6917.

Groton, CT. Fort Griswold State Park. Memorial Day through Labor Day. (203) 445-1729.

Hartford, CT. Old State House. Year-round. (203) 522-6766.

Redding, CT. Putnam Memorial State Park. Mid-April through mid-October. (203) 938-2285.

Simsbury, CT. Massacoh Plantation. May through October. (203) 658-2500.

Windsor, CT. Windsor Historical Society Museum (Fyler House). April through November. (203) 688-3813.

Concord, Lexington, MA. Minuteman National Historical Park and Lexington Historical Society houses. Park open year-round; limited access in winter. Houses open mid-April through October. Park, (508) 369-6993; Lexington houses, (508) 861-0928.

Salem, MA. House of Seven Gables. Year-round. (508) 744-0991.

Stockbridge, MA. Mission House. Late May through mid-October. (413) 298-3239.

Portsmouth, NH. Portsmouth Trail (Six houses). Seasons vary, most from June through mid-October. (603) 436-1118.

Wickford, RI. Smith's Castle. May through September. (401) 294-3521.

Bennington, VT. Bennington Battle Monument and Bennington Museum. Monument open April through October. Museum open year-round; limited hours in winter. Monument, (802) 447-0550; Museum, (802) 447-1571.

THE OVAL
OFFICE

THE ROAD FROM NEW ENGLAND TO THE OVAL OFFICE HASN'T BEEN A straight line. It has been filled with dead ends and detours, accidents and altercations.

Those who have travelled it fit into no one category. Unlike the founding fathers of Virginia or Ohio's Reconstruction era Republicans, New England-born presidents fit no one mold. Our presidents have been elected in parts of three centuries, as early as 1796 and as late as 1988. We have given to the country leaders who have brought styles and ideologies to the presidency that are 180 degrees apart: among them, the progressive and charismatic Kennedy and the austere and cool Coolidge.

We have had the Adamses, father John and son John Quincy, undiplomatic diplomats whose notable achievements were diminished in their day because of their complex and stubborn characters.

We recall the tragic tale of Franklin Pierce, who, upon his return to New Hampshire after his term as the 14th president, was shunned and hated by his fellow New Hampshirites, an individual whose greatest fault may have been living in the wrong place at the wrong time.

Two of our presidents, Chester A. Arthur and Calvin Coolidge, ascended to the presidency upon the death of an incumbent president. Arthur was not even renominated by his own party, while Coolidge was a smashing landslide in his bid to be elected. And most of us remember the brief but vibrant Kennedy administration.

The Kennedys, whose compound on Cape Cod is world famous, were not the only presidential family to be attracted to New England's cool shoreside summers. The home of one such family, the Franklin Roosevelts, still stands off the coast of Maine and can be visited by FDR faithfuls and the curious. And we can also claim a link to the president most historians regard as our best; Robert Todd Lincoln, son of Abraham Lincoln, was drawn to Vermont's mountains and built his own summer home in her hills.

Stepping inside the residences of chief executives or their families helps you understand their natures; you can get to know them as human beings rather than as remote historical figures.

JOHN AND JOHN QUINCY ADAMS

The books are stacked three and even four rows deep in this room in the home of John and John Quincy Adams, which could be called, tongue in cheek, the first presidential library.

N̲O ONE COULD ACCUSE THE ADAMSES OF GETTING TO THE WHITE HOUSE on their looks and charm.

John Adams, second president of the United States, was short, fat and prematurely bald. He felt unappreciated by his contemporaries, and this was in part justified. For a politician he let too many of his feelings show. He was brutally honest, almost rude. And he was proud. To his political enemies, this short, pudgy, pompous man was tagged, "His Rotundity."

John Quincy Adams, the sixth president and son of the second president, was an austere, corpulent figure. Calvinistic in his attitudes, he was exceedingly demanding of himself, fiercely independent, and antisocial. He lost many supporters by refusing, continuously and without conscience, to vote his party line.

But though both Adamses were disrespected, they are today regarded as two of the country's most proficient and learned statesmen. John Adams was one of the first leading colonists to call for a permanent break with Britain in the days leading up to the revolution.

Later, he helped negotiate loans from the Netherlands to aid the growth of his new country, and he played an integral role in the negotiation of the Peace Treaty of Paris in 1783. His part, though, was unfairly minimized, mainly because of the charm and grace of his compatriot, Benjamin Franklin.

Perhaps Adams's greatest accomplishment as president was the avoidance of a war with France in 1799. This deed is admired mainly in retrospect: with the majority of Americans calling for war, it likely cost Adams a second term.

John Quincy Adams, president from 1825 to 1829, was the only chief executive to win an election while not receiving a majority of either popular or electoral votes. Four candidates split the 261 electoral votes in the election of 1824, and Adams, who had finished second to Andrew Jackson, was chosen by the House of Representatives to be the sixth president of the United States. With little support from either Congress or the American citizenry for having entered the White House by the back door, he accomplished little as president, and like his father, left office feeling rather paranoid.

But like his father, John Quincy Adams was also a commendable statesman whose credits are often underrated. He spent 18 years in the House of Representatives, his terms ranging from 1830 until his death in 1848, and he stands as the only president to be elected to the House after serving as chief executive. (Adams won the election to the House without campaigning, and wrote afterwards, "No election or appointment conferred upon me ever gave me so much pleasure.")

Prior to his presidency, John Quincy Adams had served as secretary of state under President James Monroe, and ranks as one of the best who have held that position. He deserved much, but got little credit, for formulating the Monroe Doctrine.

There is a connection between some of the Adams family house furniture and the Monroe administration. Two gold Empire style chairs, known as the Monroe chairs, sit in the drawing room, or formal parlor. They were bought at a White House auction in 1861 by John Quincy's son, Charles Francis Adams, and remain in the house because Charles Francis Adams's will stipulated that no Adams heirlooms were to be removed.

Like the chairs, all the objects in the Adams house, known informally as the Old House (its official name, Peacefield, never stuck), have a story to tell, some specifically of the Adamses, others of their times. Two screens beside the fireplace in the drawing room had a specific purpose in the 19th century. It was common during that time for women to wear makeup made of beeswax; the screen reduced the heat from the fire, lessening the chance that the wax would melt and embarrass female guests. The big, airy cushions on the chairs by the fireplace were put there to accommodate the ladies' voluminous skirts, while the four-seat settee with the sewing box in the middle is a relic from the Victorian era.

Oak is abundant in the 14,000-volume library, while art is found in almost all of the dozen and a half-odd rooms, all of which are open to the public. Numerous depictions of John and Abigail Adams, John Quincy and Louisa Adams, their contemporaries and their relations hang on the many walls and feature them at various stages in their lives. Our guide told us that John Adams, subject to vanity and pride like the rest of us, placed the portrait that he felt flattered him least in the butler's pantry, the darkest part of the house; another spokesperson at the home, however, questioned the validity of that statement, saying that the original painting (the one you see is a copy) was much larger and never would have fit in the tidy wall space there.

Adams's favorite room was the study upstairs. Here sits the escritoire where he wrote his memoirs, and here also is the upholstered wing chair where he died on July 4, 1826, at age 90. No president of the United States has lived longer.

When he knew his life was about to end, Adams sighed, "Thomas Jefferson survives." Those three words proved to be his last. In the days prior to the development of speedy mass communications, there was no way he could have known that Thomas Jefferson had died earlier on that same day. The chances that the two would die on such a momentous day as July 4, 1826—the 50th anniversary of the adoption of the Declaration of Independence—are astronomical.

(The strange coincidence took another twist just five years later when the fifth president, James Monroe, also died on the Fourth of July.)

Across town are the houses where both John and John Quincy Adams were born. The two saltbox homes were built around 1680 and stand today as the oldest presidential birthplaces in existence.

John Adams's father, also named John Adams, and his mother, Susanna Boylston Adams, had four children in the recently refurbished house at 133 Franklin Street. The house next door at 141 Franklin was bequeathed to John the future president in his father's will, and it was here on July 11, 1767, that their second child and first son, John Quincy, was born.

Both birthplaces are furnished with reproductions of original pieces that sit in the Old House. In the John Quincy Adams birthplace John Adams wrote the Constitution for the Commonwealth of Massachusetts.

(A free souvenir copy is given to birthplace visitors.) A reproduction of the desk on which he wrote it can be seen here. You also will notice a variety of cooking implements by the fireplace; most people are curious about the foot toaster, which was operated by one's foot, and on chilly days might have made the foot toasty warm as well, living up to both ways its name can be interpreted. Then look high on the wall to see the eel spear, used to catch what was then considered a delicacy. It resembles a crude pitchfork to those uninitiated in colonial gourmet cuisine.

If you didn't get a chance to notice the original painting of the two birthplaces in rural Quincy which hangs in the Old House, take a glance at the copy here. A stone wall marking the property line still exists as it does in the picture, but the dirt road and pastoral setting are long gone, replaced by the paved Franklin Street and the sprawling city of Quincy.

Location: The Old House is at the corner of Adams Street and Newport Avenue in Quincy, about eight miles south of Boston. From Interstate 93 (the Southeast Expressway), take exit 8 to the Furnace Brook Parkway; take a right onto Adams Street and follow to the Old House. The address is 135 Adams Street. The birthplaces at 133 and 141 Franklin Street are south of Quincy Center. A map with directions to the birthplaces is available from any park service staff person at the Old House. **Admission** is charged. **Hours:** Every day of the week (9 AM to 5 PM), mid-April through mid-November. **Allow** an hour to an hour and a half to tour the Old House and walk the grounds. **Allow** a half hour to see the birthplaces. **Information:** Adams National Historic Site, 135 Adams Street, P.O. Box 531, Quincy, MA 02269; (617) 773-1177. **Note:** Both John and John Quincy Adams and their wives are buried in the crypt of the United First Parish Church, 1306 Hancock Street at Washington Street, Quincy. The Adamses and Woodrow Wilson, who is buried in the National Cathedral in Washington, D.C., are the only presidents buried in churches. The United First Parish Church is open every day of the week (9 AM to 5 PM) mid-April through mid-November; by appointment the remainder of the year. It is closed Thanksgiving, Christmas and New Year's Day. Donations are accepted.

FRANKLIN PIERCE

Some historians say Franklin Pierce was one of the weakest presidents in our country's history. Others believe he was just a victim of his times. Judge for yourself when you visit Hillsboro, New Hampshire's, Pierce Homestead.

IN THE REST OF THE NATION, HE MIGHT BE REFERRED TO AS FRANKLIN Who?

But in New Hampshire, Franklin Pierce is a household name.

Pierce was the 14th president of the United States and the only one of our chief executives who called New Hampshire home. He was a Democrat who served one term from March 4, 1853, to March 3, 1857.

What kind of president was he?

That depends on whose point of view you are seeking.

Most historians rank him as one of the country's worst chief executives. A survey of nearly 1,000 historians conducted by Professor Robert Murray of Pennsylvania State University in 1982 placed him 31st out of 36 presidents. Only Presidents James Buchanan, Andrew Johnson, Richard Nixon, Ulysses S. Grant and Warren G. Harding finished lower.

Pierce was a northern Democrat who supported the expansion of slavery, and regarded the growing abolitionist movement as a group of fanatic zealots who were best ignored. He signed the Kansas-Nebraska Act, which repealed the Missouri Compromise and permitted settlers in Kansas territory to decide on their own whether the state should permit slavery. Virtual civil war broke out in Kansas in the 1850s between pro) and anti-slavery supporters. Pierce was blamed for lacking the foresight to see this; to many northerners, it was an outrage!

Pierce's last years were bitter ones. When he continued to maintain his pro-slavery stand during the Civil War, most New Hampshire citizens viewed him as a traitor selling out his country. Those feelings stuck long after Pierce's death in 1869. It wasn't until 1948 that a memorial was placed over his grave in Concord, New Hampshire.

His administration was perhaps the gloomiest of any in our history. Pierce's only son, Benny—two other sons had died earlier from childhood illnesses—was killed in a train wreck just weeks prior to his inauguration. First Lady Jane Pierce, already prone to bouts of depression, became a recluse, rarely acting as official White House hostess and earning herself the name, "The Shadow in the White House."

If you visit either of Pierce's homes in Hillsboro or Concord, New Hampshire, however, you will hear a more complimentary account of the life of Franklin Pierce. He is viewed as the strict constitutionalist who stated that as president he had no power to tell the settlers of Kansas how to live. And the Franklin Pierce about whom you hear is a handsome and well-groomed son of a New Hampshire governor and a brigadier general in the Mexican War who did what was constitutionally correct and paid dearly for it.

A staff person in either house may tell you about historians who likewise defend his qualities and actions. In the August/September 1985 issue of *American Heritage*, Elting E. Morison stood by Pierce. "He tried hard to hold things together when they seemed about to fly apart—which is certainly the most obvious, and maybe, in most cases, the prudent thing to do. Though he was a good deal better than his successor, James Buchanan, he was not very good at it. Quite probably no one in those surroundings would have been good enough," conceded Morison.

Young Franklin Pierce is the one you meet in the Homestead in Hillsboro. This white clapboard home is not his birthplace. Pierce was born in a Hillsboro log cabin long since destroyed, but he moved here with his parents when just a few weeks old.

Here you get to know Pierce as a human being with a personality, rather than an abstract figure out of a history book. You meet Pierce, a college student with extracurricular activities on his mind. On one wall, there are copies of letters he wrote home from Bowdoin College in Brunswick, Maine. In one, he wrote, "I find the girls both entertaining and virtuous, if they can be both."

Family possessions reflect his privileged background. The original parlor wallpaper, printed in Paris, France, in 1822 and depicting the Bay of Naples in Italy, still hangs. In one corner of the room, actual stencilling that preceded the wallpaper is exposed.

A handsome set of china and silver rests on the dining room table downstairs. Our guide, Margaret Ellice, lead us upstairs by announcing, "You didn't have to own an English manor house to have a ballroom."

Most of the items here are period pieces, those that would have been used by a family of the Pierces' status in the early 19th century, but not necessarily owned by them, and include furniture, kitchen appliances and early daguerreotypes. As we walked by one likeness of a sour-faced older 19th-century woman, Ellice commented, "She certainly was having ulcer problems that day."

Several items that Pierce used as president were donated to the home: his sofa in the parlor; his sleigh, marked with the presidential seal; and, in an upstairs bedroom, his corset. ("Yes, it was common for men to wear them," admitted Ellice.)

But perhaps the most significant personal articles are those that belonged not to the president, but to his son, Benny. A collection of his books, featuring titles like, *Celebrated Women*, *A Glance at Philosophy*, and *Famous Indians* joins a collection of seashells in an octagonal box displayed in the parlor.

The years Pierce spent in Concord between his tenure in the Senate and as president were among his happiest. At 32, he had been the youngest senator in Washington. But at his wife's request, he resigned from the Senate in 1842 and established a private law practice.

For six years, from 1842 to 1848, Pierce lived in a two-story white Greek Revival house on Montgomery Street in Concord; and here, in the only home he would ever own, are reminders of his life as a New Hampshire lawyer.

In fact, through sundry donations from grandnieces—there are no direct descendants—and friends, the house is well stocked with actual Pierce items.

You will see Pierce's desk as soon as you enter, since the guest book for visitors to sign rests atop it. In the parlor, there is an early Victorian sofa that Jane Pierce had taken to the White House; across from that is a writing table the president used.

Other original furnishings include a cane with an ivory handle that bears the initials of the 14th president. One of the most unusual pieces is a bookcase complete with a drapery covering up the books. Our guide at the Concord home, known as the Pierce Manse, was Ruth Breton, who informed us that it was not uncommon then to be overly cautious about protecting one's books from dust.

Breton says that the Smithsonian Institution in Washington, D.C., was impressed with the multitude of Pierce belongings that you can see in the Concord home. In fact, upstairs along with a cannonball bed used by his son and a top hat worn by the president, is one of the most prized possessions tucked carefully away in a drawer—a white shirt of fine linen owned by Franklin Pierce. When you see it, you will recognize the style immediately: it looks just like all those you have observed on paintings and daguerreotypes of Victorian-era men.

The manse was sold upon Pierce's return from the Mexican War in 1848. And today, it no longer sits on Montgomery Street. An urban renewal project in 1966 threatened the home with destruction, and it was through the efforts of the Concord-based Pierce Brigade that it was saved. In 1971, it was moved to its present location at 14 Penacook Street at the northern end of Main Street.

Pierce and his wife are buried in Concord's Old North Cemetery.

Location: The Franklin Pierce Homestead is three miles west of the center of Hillsboro, on Route 31 near its junction with Route 9. The Pierce Manse in Concord is at 14 Penacook Street at the northern end of Main Street; it is located about one mile north of the State House. **Admission** is charged to both houses. **Hours:** The Franklin Pierce Homestead is open Memorial Day through Columbus Day. It is open weekdays in July and August, weekends only during the rest of their season. The Pierce Manse is open June through Labor Day weekend, Monday through Friday, closed July 4 and Labor Day. **Allow** a half hour to 40 minutes to see each house. **Information:** Hillsboro Historical Society, P.O. Box 896, Hillsboro, NH 03244, (603) 478-3165 or 478-3913. Pierce Manse, P.O. Box 425, Concord, NH 03302, (603) 224-7668 or 225-2068. **Note:** The Franklin Pierce Homestead is presently undergoing a major restoration to make it more historically accurate. But most construction work is being done off-season and the house is open as usual.

ROBERT TODD LINCOLN

Courtesy: Hildene

Robert Todd Lincoln planned to use the 412-acre estate amid the mountains of Vermont as a haven from business worries. But he ended up conducting business from his home, Hildene, for most of his 22 summers here.

THERE IS A LINK TO THE LINCOLNS IN NEW ENGLAND.

It's not to Abraham, product of Kentucky, Indiana and Illinois, but to his son, Robert Todd Lincoln, who moved into a Manchester, Vermont, mansion in 1905 and used it as a summer home through 1926. The spacious home, called Hildene, was last occupied by a Lincoln descendant in 1975 and was formally opened to the public four years later.

People visit Hildene for different reasons. Some are bona fide Lincoln buffs who can already claim Abraham Lincoln's log cabin birthplace in Kentucky; his Indiana boyhood home; his Springfield, Illinois, residence; and even Ford's Theatre in Washington, D.C., to their sightseeing credit. Others come simply to see a gracious old mansion that has been lovingly restored. Still others—including Nordic skiers, for whom Hildene provides a cross-country ski center—are drawn by the dominant Green Mountains which fringe Manchester and surround the home at every angle.

First Lady Mary Todd Lincoln enjoyed the scenery as well. She and her children first came here in 1863, returned the following year, and had plans to come back with the president in 1865. But the assassination of President Lincoln on April 14 of that year changed the plans.

There would be more tragedies to haunt the Lincolns. Three of their four children, all sons, would die before reaching their adult years. Only Robert Todd, the eldest, survived childhood.

His 82 years were filled with noteworthy accomplishments. He had graduated from Harvard University in 1864 and was commissioned a captain in the Army, joining General Ulysses S. Grant's staff; he had been at Appomattox on April 9, 1865, when General Robert E. Lee surrendered to Grant. Five days later, he went back to the White House, electing to stay home while his parents attended the presentation of "Our American Cousin" at Ford's Theatre. He never forgave himself for staying home.

By the time Robert Todd Lincoln died in 1926, he was a millionaire, having earned his fortune as a Chicago lawyer and an executive (president and chairman of the board) of the Pullman Palace Car Company. He also served a stint as a statesman. President James A. Garfield appointed him secretary of war and he served at this post from 1881 through the administration of Chester A. Arthur, the Vermont-born president who succeeded Garfield following his assassination. Later, in Benjamin Harrison's administration, he served as minister to Great Britain.

Robert Todd Lincoln had been walking with President Garfield in the Baltimore and Potomac railroad station when Charles J. Guiteau, a mentally unstable man who had been seeking an appointment as consul to Paris, vented his anger and frustration by shooting the president. Garfield died two and one-half months later.

Curiously, Lincoln had stepped off a train in Buffalo, New York, on September 6, 1901, just as President William McKinley was fatally shot by anarchist Leon F. Czolgosz only a few miles away at the 1901 World's Fair, called the Pan-American Exposition. Add to this string of coincidences the fact that President Kennedy's body reposed on the same East Room catafalque used for Lincoln's, and Robert Todd Lincoln is buried a few hundred feet from President Kennedy. Thus, in a morbid twist of fate, Lincoln shares a direct connection with all four assassinated presidents.

It was at age 62 during the presidency of Theodore Roosevelt that Lincoln, lured by his law partner, moved to Manchester. After his death nearly 21 years later, his granddaughter moved into the house, and her possessions are also seen on a tour through the home.

Robert Lincoln's bedroom and library are perhaps the most revealing of his character. The bedroom was originally a den, but Lincoln converted it in 1908 and seldom went upstairs. In the library, where he did most of his work running the Pullman Company, you will see original furnishings, such as the little coal stove, the rose-colored drapes and the furniture with rose-colored upholstery. The resemblance of this room to the interior of a Pullman car may not be coincidence.

But just about every visitor, including those who care little about history, find the 1,000-pipe Aeolian organ fascinating. This 1908 instrument is claimed to be the oldest residential organ with player attachment in the country. (Following an article on Hildene in *Americana*, a reader wrote a letter to the editor in the magazine's September/October 1983 issue taking issue with that claim, however.) Regardless of whether or not there is an older one elsewhere, this is a beauty! A professional organ restorer, with some help from Hildene volunteers, took two years to dismantle, clean, repair and reassemble the harmonic masterpiece. If you are lucky, you will be able to hear it being played when you visit.

Since Robert Lincoln rarely ventured upstairs in this 24-room Georgian Revival mansion, the second study is filled with items owned by Peggy Beckwith, his granddaughter, who lived here for 37 years. She was a woman whose talents and interests were widespread. At various times, she could be found milking cows, painting in oils, listening to her record player, or flying her own biplane. Her parachute, Bing Crosby records, and unfinished paintings testify to the different ways she spent her time.

Location: Hildene is on Route 7A, about one and a half miles south of Manchester. **Admission** is charged. **Hours:** Mid-May through late October, daily. **Allow** an hour and a half to two hours to tour the house and walk around the extensive grounds. **Information:** Hildene, Box 377, Manchester Village, VT 05254, (802) 362-1788. **Note:** Picnic tables are on the grounds. The villages of Manchester and nearby Manchester Center offer many fine craft and import shops. The grounds are open in winter for cross-country skiing.

CALVIN COOLIDGE AND CHESTER A. ARTHUR

It was at this modest living room table that Calvin Coolidge was sworn in by his father as President of the United States.

SOME SAY THAT THE BIRTHPLACE AND BOYHOOD HOMES OF PRESIDENTS reflect both their personalities and their administrative policies. Lyndon Johnson's simple dogtrot farmhouse birthplace in the Texas hill country symbolizes his earthy, rustic manner.

Others disagree and point to the case of Theodore Roosevelt. His plush Victorian brownstone near Gramercy Park in New York City contradicts his reputation as a thorn in the side of turn-of-the-century robber barons and as a hearty environmentalist to whom the wide open spaces of the American West beckoned, attributes more appropriately at home at his Sagamore Hill on Long Island. And many visitors find it hard to associate the patrician setting of Hyde Park with Franklin D. Roosevelt's liberal New Deal.

Vermont has ammunition for both sides. Plymouth Notch boasts the tidy birthplace and no-frills boyhood home of the 30th president, Calvin Coolidge, the epitome of the stoic and frugal Yankee.

Further up in the state in North Fairfield is a replica of the cabin in which the 21st president, Chester A. Arthur, lived as an infant. Despite his humble entrance into the world, Arthur was a debonair, high-living chief executive, who hired renowned New York designer Louis Tiffany to completely renovate the White House to suit his tastes.

Both homes are run by the Vermont Division for Historic Preservation and are open to the public.

History was made in the tiny village of Plymouth Notch on the night of August 3, 1923, when in the family sitting room, a father swore his son in as president of the United States. Vice President Calvin Coolidge was summering at his boyhood home on the family farm when he received word via a Western Union office in Bridgewater, Vermont, that President Warren G. Harding had just died.

No president before or since has been sworn into office in his own home, and certainly, not by his own father. The family sitting room, now known as the oath of office room, looks much as it did that historic night. A little table is arranged with a pen, a Bible, a small stack of papers and a single kerosene lamp. The scene is dramatic in its simplicity.

Contrast this room with the one next to it. Here is another, more formal, parlor. Typically, this one was rarely used. If it were not for the long Vermont winter, it might have been entered only once or twice a year, but because of the cost of heating the Union Christian Church across the street, Sunday services were occasionally conducted here.

You can't forget that this is a backwoods farmhouse as you wander through the narrow corridor, passing the tool room, the laundry room, and the woodshed. It was young Cal Coolidge's job to split wood for the kitchen stove, and you can still see the darkened box used to smoke hams outdoors. The fire for smoking was kindled in an iron kettle.

More indoor cooking kettles rest in the kitchen and the pantry. A trapdoor under the counter opens on a barrel of flour stored underneath.

The Coolidge kitchen sink is made of iron, and the future president's mother used to wash it with kerosene to protect it against rust. A pumice stone for cleaning steel knives lies next to the silver-polishing box on the drain board.

Although he ate most of his meals here, Calvin's lasting memories were not of warm family dinners and casual conversations. With uncharacteristic openness, the president wrote several years later, "The hardest thing in the world for me was to have to go through that kitchen door and greet the visitors. By fighting hard, I used to manage to get through that kitchen door. I'm all right now with old friends, but every time I meet a stranger, I have to stand by the old kitchen door a minute. It's hard."

Further down the corridor is the crude two-hole wooden privy. Reading material includes an *Old Farmer's Almanac,* a Sears and Roebuck catalogue, and a bundle of seed catalogues. In an age when recent presidents have kept plush ranches and seaside mansions as their homes away from the White House, most visitors find it hard to believe that this was the only toilet facility in "the summer White House" until former President Coolidge built an extension in 1932, less than a year before he died.

Across the street is the Union Christian Church, built in 1849, the regular place of worship for generations of Coolidges. It is still the Coolidge family church during warm weather. John Coolidge, octogenarian son of the president, attends when he is in residence in a nearby house.

John, a conservative Republican like his father, owns the Plymouth Cheese Company up the road from the historic home; you are invited to step inside the company building, a wood-frame structure typical of this part of New England, to browse or purchase some farm-fresh Vermont cheese.

The president's boyhood home is not the only attraction here. His actual birthplace is across the street in a modest house attached to the general store. The Wilder Barn holds old sleighs and farming equipment. And there is the visitors' center. Coolidge was the last president not to have a presidential library-museum complex, but this stone visitors' center, well-planned and enjoyable, portrays Coolidge's life through photographs, furnishings, and political cartoons. To make the most out of your visit, stop here first.

Finally, there is Plymouth Cemetery where the president is buried. Coolidge often said that he came from the people; this humility is exemplified by his simple marker. The stone does not even mention that he was president of the United States; all that is noted is his name, date of death, and the date of his birth, which appropriately, was the Fourth of July, 1872.

Vermont claims another president. Chester A. Arthur was born near the Canadian border in 1829. The only time he stood for election was as a tag-along vice-presidential candidate with James A. Garfield in 1880. Just six months after taking office, Garfield died; and it is said that a prominent Republican, upon hearing the news, yelled out, "Chet Arthur—president of the United States? Good God!"

After all, Arthur had been disgraced just three years earlier when, in an effort to clean up partisanship and corruption, he was fired as Collector of the Port of New York.

But the record shows that Arthur was a fairly good president. One of his greatest accomplishments was signing into law an overdue civil service act that helped promote governmental reform.

He is also credited with beginning the reconstruction of the United States Navy, which led to its victorious role in the 1898 Spanish-American War. But despite his achievements, Arthur couldn't win the respect of his own party and was denied the nomination for president in 1884. Today, he is a virtual non-entity among American chief executives, the "Rodney Dangerfield" of presidents. A guide at the Chester A. Arthur home doesn't hide that fact. "Poor old Chester," she laments. "He's not remembered by anyone today."

The modest cabin was built in 1954 as a replica of Arthur's 1830 home, which, at the time, was thought to be his birthplace. The likeness was based on an old photograph. Later research proved that Arthur was actually born in 1829, and not in the building shown in the photo, which today is considered a copy of Arthur's home as an infant.

For years it was furnished as a home typical of its time, with an old rope bed, a kitchen stove and a crude wooden nightstand. Unfortunately, the building was picked clean by thieves in 1985 and wasn't reopened until September, 1989. Inside it now is a mounted interpretive exhibit, full of old photographs, political cartoons and posted commentary, discussing the man, his administration, and early 19th century Vermont.

Arthur's father was a Baptist minister, and the family was constantly on the move. The boy lived here only two years, then was shuttled to different parts of the state until his family settled in Albany, New York, where he grew up. Except for a brief residence near Bennington, he never returned to Vermont and spent most of his adult life in New York City. He is buried in Albany.

Location: To reach the Coolidge Homestead from the south, take Interstate 91, exit 6, onto Route 103 north to Route 100 north to Route 100A and follow the signs. **Admission** is charged. **Hours:** Mid-May to mid-October, daily. **Allow** one to two hours to tour the boyhood home and the other buildings on the grounds (where there are picnic tables).

Location: To reach the Arthur home from Interstate 89, take exit 19 onto Route 104 north to Route 36 east and follow the signs; the road becomes dirt a few miles before you reach the home. **Admission** is free. **Hours:** June to mid-October, Wednesday through Sunday. **Allow** a half hour to an hour.

Information for both the Coolidge and Arthur sites: The Vermont Division for Historic Preservation, 135 State Street Drawer 33, Montpelier, VT 05602, (802) 828-3226.

Note: A picnic area is on the grounds. The North Fairfield Baptist Church, where Arthur's father preached, is nearby and open to the public. Ask for details when visiting the home.

FRANKLIN D. ROOSEVELT

Photo by Michael Schuman

*This was the summer cottage of the Franklin D. Roosevelt family. It made a
lonely little island off the coast of Maine a household word.*

A BRIEF DIP IN THE CHILLY WATER OF A BAY BY A NEW YORK ATTORNEY
named Franklin Delano Roosevelt put an otherwise unassuming island
named Campobello onto the front pages and into the hearts of men and
women across the world.

The island, off the coast of Maine in Passamaquoddy Bay, part of New
Brunswick, Canada, was the summer home of the James Roosevelt family. Son Franklin vacationed regularly here with his family from the time
he was an infant until his 39th year.

On August 10, 1921, Franklin took a swim in warm Lake Glensevern
prior to diving into the ice-chilled water of the Bay of Fundy. The Roosevelt family had spent the day on their yacht, the *Vireo;* Franklin usually
ended such an excursion with a little vigorous aquatic exercise.

But as he returned to the house from his swim, the 39-year-old Roosevelt sensed something wrong. He later wrote, "When I reached the
house, the mail was in with several newspapers I hadn't seen. I sat
reading for a while, too tired even to dress."

Courtesy: Franklin D. Roosevelt Library

Franklin D. Roosevelt with daughter Anna at Campobello.

After a few hours of reading, he began to feel chills, which became so uncomfortable that he skipped dinner and went to bed. After a restless night, Franklin discovered he had a fever. He scoffed at any suggestion that he had anything more severe than a bad cold, or perhaps a minor case of lumbago.

But the symptoms worsened. He had trouble moving his left leg while climbing out of bed. As the day progressed, he began to lose all movement in his leg; by afternoon, the right leg felt as paralyzed as the left.

Two medical experts, the family's summer physician and a nationally known Philadelphia doctor who was vacationing in Bar Harbor, Maine, misdiagnosed the case. One prescribed massage, and for two weeks Franklin's wife, Eleanor, and his friend and advisor, Louis Howe, provided him with the prescribed treatment. The only result was an increase in agonizing pain.

When Dr. Robert D. Lovett, an orthopedics specialist from Newport, Rhode Island, arrived on August 25, 15 days after the initial symptoms, he diagnosed Roosevelt's ailment as infantile paralysis; and he said that the two weeks of constant massage had only made the affliction worse.

Less than a year earlier, Franklin D. Roosevelt had run for vice president of the United States with James Cox on the Democratic ticket in the 1920 general election. They lost to Republicans Warren G. Harding and Calvin Coolidge in what still stands as the biggest landslide in terms of popular vote in the history of the country. The Cox-Roosevelt ticket received 34.2 percent of the vote to the Republicans' 60.4 percent.

Roosevelt had been hoping to run for governor of New York in 1922, but these plans were suddenly scrapped. His main concern was his future as a healthy human being, with political goals secondary.

The appealing stage play and movie, "Sunrise at Campobello," dramatized this story, concluding with the 1928 Democratic convention where Roosevelt, played by Ralph Bellamy, walked with hidden leg braces across the stage to begin his speech nominating Al Smith for president.

"Sunrise" made Campobello almost a household word. The very name symbolized FDR's courage and determination, qualities which spurred him on to become one of the most successful statesmen in history. After serving two terms as governor of New York from 1928 to 1932, he was elected to an unprecedented four terms as president before his death in office on April 12, 1945.

Whether or not your own political views agree with his, Roosevelt is regarded, with Lincoln, as one of the country's two greatest presidents.

The family's Dutch colonial summer cottage (a "cottage" which had 18 bedrooms) is the focal point of Roosevelt Campobello International Park, a unique joint memorial operated by both the United States and Canada.

A film about the life of FDR and specifically his life on Campobello is shown regularly in the visitor center; watch it to gain background and to appreciate the man's relation with this island before heading over to the cottage. (You may think you are familiar with the Roosevelt presidency, but we'll bet you will learn at least something new about his administration or his life by watching the film.)

If you have seen FDR's famous "Big House" at Hyde Park, New York, the Campobello home might surprise you. Where formal, bulky Victorian furnishings dominate Hyde Park, the vacation home interior is light and airy. Wicker is the rule here, with tables and chairs resembling redistributed baskets. The family wicker picnic basket sits in the butler's pantry, and a wicker fishing basket accompanies a deerskin rug—made from a deer which FDR shot while hunting nearby—in a downstairs bedroom. Adding to the gossamery effect are translucent curtains covering the windows in most rooms in the house.

A schoolroom in which the Roosevelt children, known as "the chicks" to their father, were given private lessons has been converted into a small museum, offering further insight into the leisure-time life-style of young FDR in the early years of this century.

Many of his belongings reflect his love for all things nautical, including a model sailboat. Nearby is a spyglass, used to view yachts on the horizon, and a megaphone that Franklin employed to amplify his voice and which was often used to call the children in at mealtime.

FDR returned here only three times after he contracted polio. His son, Franklin D. Roosevelt, Jr., has suggested that Campobello was too depressing for the wheelchair-bound president because it brought back too many memories of his young and active life. A wooden chair with a canvas seat, constructed with four handles specifically to carry Roosevelt during a 1933 visit, is in the museum, a mute reminder of the bittersweet moment when he came back to his summer home for the first time since he had left on a stretcher some 12 years earlier, calling out to his family as he was being carried to a waiting boat, "Don't worry, kids. I'll see you soon."

Location: Campobello Island, New Brunswick, is located across the Franklin D. Roosevelt Memorial Bridge from Lubec, Maine. After you cross the bridge, bear to the left until you reach the Roosevelt Home. **Admission** is free. **Hours:** Memorial Day weekend through the next 20 weeks, daily. **Allow** two hours to tour the home, see the film and walk the grounds. **Information:** Roosevelt Campobello International Park, P.O. Box 97, Lubec, ME 04652, (506) 752-2922. **Note:** You have to go through customs to enter Campobello Island, which might be a nuisance but is rarely time-consuming. Keep in mind that Campobello is in the Atlantic Time Zone, one hour ahead of Eastern Time. While on the island, you might want to take the time to see some of the other sights, including Hubbard Cottage, also on the grounds of Roosevelt Campobello International Park. Natural sights worth seeing include Friar's Head, Wilson's Beach and Herring Cove Beach. Hiking and other outdoor recreation opportunities are available throughout the island and picnic facilities are available both inside and outside the park.

JOHN F. KENNEDY

Courtesy: John F. Kennedy Library/Museum

A concrete and steel time capsule, the John F. Kennedy Library and Museum stands nine stories high and was dedicated on October 20, 1979.

AN ADMIRER ONCE ASKED PRESIDENT JOHN F. KENNEDY, "HOW DID you become a war hero?"

"It was involuntary," the chief executive modestly responded. "They sank my boat."

Some years later, the president's mother, Rose Kennedy, reminisced about her offspring and their resistance to certain childhood routines. "The children did not do too well with their piano lessons," she recalled. "Radio was a new thing then and they said that people wouldn't want to listen to them play when they could hear the same songs on the radio."

At two locations in the Boston metropolitan area, you will find evidence of a charismatic president's sense of humor and of his caring mother's memories.

At his birthplace in Brookline, now part of the national park system and called the John F. Kennedy National Historic Site, you see many original Kennedy possessions in six rooms and hear in each a brief taped commentary by Rose Kennedy.

The Kennedy Library and Museum, located at Columbia Point in Boston's Dorchester section, chronicles JFK's life through well-placed and neatly organized exhibits in an eye-catching modern building.

The piano that the young Kennedys avoided is in the living room of the Beals Street birthplace, restored to its 1917 appearance. The piano was originally a wedding gift, and although the youngsters wouldn't oblige, Rose remarks that she often played at Christmas while the family sang carols.

Holidays, she continues, were important to young marrieds Joe and Rose Kennedy at this three-story frame house. In the dining room, you hear that they made a point of talking about the significance of each holiday over family dinners. After church on Sunday, they discussed the Gospel, and the children soon realized that unless they paid attention, they would be drilled again on the same subject the following Sunday.

The future president was born May 29, 1917, at 3 P.M. on the twin bed nearest the window in the master bedroom upstairs. Hospital births weren't yet routine, and that bed was chosen because it gave the doctor the best light. Across the hall in the nursery are the bassinet and christening dress used by the children.

The Kennedys didn't stay here long; they had bought this house, then five years old, in 1914, and moved to a bigger residence in the same neighborhood in 1921.

It's easy to say that the Kennedy Library and Museum picks up where the birthplace leaves off, but that's not totally accurate. The displays actually pre-date the birthplace, carrying the president's family history back to the marriage of his grandfather in East Boston in 1849, and forward to Senator Robert F. Kennedy's assassination in 1968.

Through the use of a superb time line coupling major Kennedy family events with important world and national occurrences, even people bored by history are enthralled.

"We don't want the exhibits just to say what we have. We want them to tell what we have to say," states Dan Fenn, director of the presidential complex. Fenn hopes that the museum teaches as well as catches your eye, citing the exhibit on Kennedy's 1946 Congressional campaign as a political lesson.

Memory-joggers abound as, depending on your age, you either relive or discover for the first time the newsmaking events of the Kennedy years, their importance subtly underlined. The Cuban missile crisis ("The greatest danger of all," President Kennedy said, "would be to do nothing"), the Peace Corps, Berlin—they all come back through the use of photographs, newspaper headlines, campaign posters, films and other forms of memorabilia.

Although they might seem that way, the president's three years in the White House were not always one crisis after another after another. A blackthorn walking stick Kennedy received during a trip to Ireland is grandly displayed. So is the gown Jackie Kennedy wore at the inauguration gala, plus congratulatory telegrams and tickets to the 1961 inauguration. Can you guess what a reserved seat at the inaugural parade cost? Try $3. Times have changed.

John F. Kennedy, the man, is recalled not only for his actions but for his attributes, specifically his spirit of adventure and humor. He was a former Navy man and, like Franklin Roosevelt, was infatuated with the sea and its brisk, briny life. He reflected these tastes in his hobbies; the detailed scrimshaw and the intricate ship models are worthy of admiration regardless of one's political opinions.

The world-famous Kennedy humor comes through in a series of videotaped highlights of his press conferences. A sample:

"How's your aching back?" a reporter called out in one clip.

"It depends on the weather," the president calmly responded, "political and otherwise."

You may recall the famed rocking chair where he rested that aching back. It's now part of the most poignant exhibit here. A replica of his White House desk as he left it when he departed for Dallas, Texas, on November 21, 1963, occupies a central portion of the museum. In front of the desk is the familiar old rocking chair.

Location: John F. Kennedy National Historic Site is at 83 Beals Street, Brookline. It can be reached by taking the North Station/Storrow Drive exit off Interstate 93 (the Southeast Expressway). Take the Kenmore Square/Fenway exit off Storrow Drive and at Kenmore Square, follow Beacon Street (be careful—it's a tricky intersection) all the way to Harvard Street. Take a right onto Harvard Street, then the fourth right onto Beals Street. The house is marked with an American flag and a plaque. **Admission** is charged. **Hours:** Year-round, daily; closed Thanksgiving, Christmas, New Year's Day. **Allow** a half hour. **Information:** John F. Kennedy National Historic Site, 83 Beals Street, Brookline, MA 02146, (617) 566-7937.

Location: The Kennedy Library and Museum in Dorchester can be reached by taking Interstate 93 (the Southeast Expressway) to exit 17 and following the signs. **Admission** is charged. **Hours:** Year-round, daily; closed Thanksgiving, Christmas, New Year's Day. **Allow** one and a half to three hours. **Information:** John F. Kennedy Library, Columbia Point, Dorchester, MA 02125, (617) 929-4523.

MUSEUM OF AMERICAN POLITICAL LIFE

*This torchlight parade orator at the Museum of American Political Life bears a
strong resemblance to turn-of-the-century populist William Jennings Bryan.*

IF YOU THINK *THE WIZARD OF OZ* IS NOTHING MORE THAN A CHILDREN'S
story, you owe yourself a visit to the Museum of American Political Life
at the University of Hartford. At this new attraction in West Hartford,
Connecticut, the wholly American fetishes of politics and politicking are
put under a magnifying glass; even *The Wizard* will be seen from a whole
new perspective.

It is here that visitors can admire over 1,500 political mementoes,
ranging from George Washington's inaugural buttons to nylon stockings
bearing the phrase, "I Like Ike," as well as a JFK lapel ornament in the
shape of a PT boat.

Someone once said selling politicians is no different than selling soap. Here you will find out how true this statement is. Do you think carefully manicured image-making of presidential candidates is something new? At the museum you will discover that this practice is 150 years old. In addition you will discover how an argument about refrigerators played an integral role in Richard Nixon's 1960 campaign and why George Bush wasn't photographed at Kennebunkport prior to the 1988 election.

This museum opened in May, 1989 (the bicentennial year of the American Presidency) on the campus of the University of Hartford. The nucleus of the museum is the DeWitt Collection of Presidential Americana, some 40,000 political mementoes saved for over forty years by Travelers Insurance Companies executive J. Doyle DeWitt. Today the total museum collection approaches 60,000 pieces.

Museum Director Professor Edmund B. Sullivan calls the Museum of American Political Life, "the thinking person's museum." If your cerebral impulses can be stimulated by examining the workings of a wind-up Jimmy Carter Peanut doll or being reminded of the choices offered by the 1988 primaries, you will enjoy your visit to this museum. You can spend your time here analyzing, remembering or getting sentimental for times long past, when a torchlight parade was the most anticipated event of the year.

Memories are most vividly kindled by the History Wall, which consists of a massive time line that covers the entire 70-foot-long east wall and connects the administrations of George Washington and George Bush. Adjacent to the History Wall is a 70-foot-long display case bursting with nearly 1,000 campaign buttons, ribbons, leaflets, bumper stickers, auto license plates and anything else that sports a politico's name or a catchy slogan. Buttons especially are in profusion. Expect to find scores bearing a wide gamut of sentiments. There are some for Democrats ("I'm Just Wild About Harry"); for Republicans ("We Don't Want Eleanor Either"); for third party supporters ("Gus Hall for President—Vote Communist"), for also-rans ("Right From the Start—Kemp in '88), and for alarmists ("MacArthur—Win or Die").

The showcase exhibit in the museum is the life-sized torchlight parade, a symbol of grass roots politics, American ingenuity and the day when your grandparents' grandparents were children.

What was a torchlight parade? During the last 30 years of the 19th century, campaign speeches were often followed by massive marches. The marchers would dress in vibrant uniforms and carry flaming torches. They were often followed by firefighting equipment, a cornet band, fireworks wagons and local dignitaries. In the midst of it all was the candidate.

Says Director Sullivan, "It was a different story a century ago. Few

Americans ever saw a president. Even those who couldn't vote took part in torchlight parades. We're more like spectators today. There are too many diversions."

A total of 17 life-sized mannequins, well-dressed and holding signs and torches comprise the parade. It begins on the entrance level and winds down a spiral staircase to the main floor where another mannequin dressed as a "Gay 90s" candidate, arms raised in the midst of vivid oratory, speaks to the crowd. Accompanying the life-sized parade diorama is "Ready for the Parade," an exhibit filled with fancy torches in the shapes of animals, hats, and stars.

The parade speaker bears a strong resemblance to turn-of-the-century populist William Jennings Bryan although Director Sullivan maintains that the bald-headed man with the bow tie and vest is meant to represent any archetypical 19-century politician.

It is, however, acknowledged that Bryan was indeed the basis for the character of the cowardly lion in *The Wizard of Oz*, the children's novel that wasn't just for children. *Oz* author L. Frank Baum was a turn-of-the-century prairie populist and Democrat who endorsed Bryan and marched in his torchlight parades when Bryan ran for President against William McKinley in 1896.

According to one exhibit, Baum's allegory was as follows: Dorothy (the average American citizen) ventures to the Emerald City (Washington, D.C.) by way of the yellow brick road which represents the gold standard. After losing her magical silver shoes (the silver standard—though her shoes are red in the famous movie, they are silver in the book), Dorothy encounters a scarecrow (the American farmer), a tin man (the eastern industrial worker), and the cowardly lion (Bryan, who Baum felt lacked courage). In the end, populism is defeated and Dorothy returns to Kansas.

One major section in the museum is called, "From Log Cabin to White House"; it is here that you will learn how presidential candidates are sold like soap. Made-for-television political ads are presented on monitors for your viewing pleasure and you can see Richard Nixon depicted as a friend to law and order and Barry Goldwater portrayed as a man who could start World War III.

Wall displays also afford a look at the packaging of candidates. A political ad from the 1960 campaign was meant to portray Richard Nixon as tough on defense. It features a photograph of a determined Nixon poking a finger at Soviet Premier Nikita Khrushchev with the accompanying words, "Nixon Speaks With Authority. He stands for courage."

According to Director Sullivan, "The photo was taken at the 1959 Moscow Trade Fair and Nixon was saying, 'Our refrigerators are better than yours.' "

Image-making began in earnest during the election of 1840 when the country was suffering through its first significant depression. Martin Van Buren was the incumbent running for a second term against Whig party candidate William Henry Harrison, whose supporters portrayed Van Buren as a champagne-drinking aristocrat living in the lap of luxury. In the display case accompanying the History Wall is an early Whig advertisement depicting a smiling Van Buren "with a beautiful goblet of White House champagne." At the same time, the Whigs praised Harrison as a man of the people. A fired clay log cabin on view, a relic from 1840, was used to promote the claim that Harrison was born poor in a log cabin.

In fact, William Henry Harrison was one of a long line of Virginia blue bloods and was born at Berkeley, a palatial James River plantation. At the time of the campaign, he was living very well on a prosperous Ohio farm. In November, he defeated Van Buren at the polls.

That wasn't the last time such a campaign tactic was used.

As Director Sullivan points out, "That's why George Bush would never go to Kennebunkport for photos prior to the (1988) election. He needed the blue collar vote."

Whoever said, "The more things change, the more things remain the same.", must have been in politics.

Location: From Interstate 84, exit onto Prospect Avenue (exit 44) and follow it to its end. Turn right onto Albany Avenue, then a sharp left onto Bloomfield Avenue (Route 189). The campus is a half mile on the right. The museum is in the University Center along with the Joseloff Gallery and the Mortensen Library; signs are not well-placed, so watch carefully. You can park in G lot on weekends and when school is not in session. At other times, park in L lot. **Admission** is charged. **Hours:** Year-round, closed Sunday and Monday. **Allow** an hour to 90 minutes for those casually interested, up to three hours if you are a political or history buff. **Information:** The Museum of American Political Life, University of Hartford, West Hartford, CT 06117; (203) 243-4090.

OTHER SITES

Here are some other new england sites open to the public that have associations with American presidents.

Weymouth, MA. Abigail Adams House. Birthplace of Abigail Smith Adams, wife of John Adams and mother of John Quincy Adams. Summer season. (617) 335-1067.

Northampton, MA. Calvin Coolidge Memorial Room in Forbes Library. Collection of photographs, correspondence and memorabilia relating to the 30th president of the United States. Year-round. (413) 584-8399.

Newport, RI, Hammersmith Farm. Summer retreat during the Kennedy administration; President Kennedy came here for days at a time, once spending as much as a month. Jacqueline Bouvier, stepdaughter of owner Hugh D. Auchinloss, Jr., made her debut here and the wedding reception following her marriage to Kennedy was held here. April through mid-November. (401) 846-0420.

Other presidents as well as some of our own lived in New England in homes that are no longer standing or are privately owned and not open to the public. For example:

James A. Garfield, a native of Ohio whose family came from the Monadnock area of New Hampshire, attended Williams College in Williamstown, Massachusetts. He later taught for a short time in North Pownal, across the border in Vermont. When he was shot, he had been about to board a train to his college reunion in Williamstown.

Grover Cleveland was born in New Jersey and made his political career in New York. His summer White House was "Grey Gables," a two-story cottage at Buzzards Bay on Cape Cod. It continued to be his summer home after he left the White House; the house was sold after his daughter, Ruth, died in 1904. He spent his next summer in Tamworth, New Hampshire, which is now the home of his son, Francis Grover Cleveland, born in 1903 and founder of the famous Barnstormers summer theatrical group.

William Howard Taft, born in Cincinnati to a family with roots in Townshend and Taftsville, Vermont, taught at Yale University after leaving the Oval Office. In office, he visited Robert Todd Lincoln's "Hildene" and played golf in Manchester, Vermont. His residences in New Haven, Connecticut, from 1913 to 1921 included: 367 Prospect Street (a Romanesque mansion called "Hillcrest"); a home at 70 Grove Street, since destroyed; 113 Whitney Avenue; and 60 York Avenue. He left Yale when named chief justice of the Supreme Court in 1921 by President Warren G. Harding.

Woodrow Wilson, a native of Virginia who grew up in other southern states and made his career in New Jersey, taught at Wesleyan University in Middletown, Connecticut, from 1888–1890. He lived in a colonial house on High Street. Ironically, the bespectacled pedagogue coached one season of college football while at Wesleyan, before becoming president of Princeton. As president, he sometimes made the Cornish, New Hampshire, estate of Winston Churchill, the American novelist, his "Summer White House."

Calvin Coolidge, though born in Vermont, made his career as a lawyer and politician in Massachusetts. His Northampton homes at 21 Massasoit Street (1905–1930) and 16 Hampton Terrace (called "The Beeches," where he lived from 1930–1933) are privately owned.

John F. Kennedy, lived at 122 Bowdoin Street on Beacon Hill in Boston while a Congressman in the late 1940s and early 1950s. The famous Kennedy compound, summer residence during the White House years, stands at Irving and Marchant Avenues at Hyannis Port on Cape Cod. It is still owned by the Kennedy family. Within walking distance of Kennedy's birthplace is his boyhood home at the northeast corner of Abbottsford and Naples Roads. Here the future president lived from 1921 until 1927. The house is privately owned and closed to the public. The Kennedy family church and two of the Kennedy boys' schools are also within walking distance. A brochure detailing a walking tour of John Kennedy's boyhood neighborhood is available at the birthplace.

George Bush was born in a Victorian home his parents were renting at 173 Adams Street in Milton, Massachusetts. His parents moved to Greenwich, Connecticut when George was six months old, where he grew up in a Tudor style home at 11 Stanwick Street and a wood frame house at 15 Grove Street near the Boston Post Road. The Milton and Greenwich homes still stand but are privately owned and not open to the public.

The Bush family compound which doubles as the Summer White House is on Walker's Point in Kennebunkport, Maine. It is closed to the public, but you can see it by taking Route 9 (Wells Road) in Kennebunkport to Ocean Avenue and following to Walker's Point. The compound sits across a cove on a neck jutting into the gulf.

WORKING IN NEW ENGLAND

W E HAVE BUILT BOATS AND SAILED THEM, AT TIMES TO FIGHT BATTLES, at times to import treasures. Our farms have produced milk and maple syrup while our factories were churning out textiles and tools. Monuments and mansions across America are made from New England granite and marble.

New England has never been handicapped by a one-resource economy. Unlike the Pacific Northwest with its timber, and Michiganders with their automobiles, our business and industry have been varied, which explains why, in periods of recessions and inflation, our economic status remains stable and our unemployment rates relatively low.

For the daytripper, our potpourri of vocations makes for fascinating travel. Regardless of our state of residence, there are attractions open to the public which illustrate long-standing ways of earning a living in New England.

Some are no longer primary industries. At least not here. The world of the textile mill worker that you can explore in Lowell and Pawtucket is a relic. Many of the textile manufacturers have long since left New England for the Southeast, only to leave later for the Far East. No person working in a 19th-century mill would have considered his or her labor romantic. But sentimentalists in our day often turn maudlin when hearing the tales of the mill girls with their wide-eyed dreams or while admiring the regimented rows of industrial brick that stand like sentinels guarding our rivers and canals.

Other industries continue to thrive here, reflecting long-standing traditions and ways of life that persist despite the onslaught of hi-tech. Although it's usually considered rude to look over another's shoulder while that person is hard at work, you are welcome to do so as skilled craftspersons polish marble or farm hands boil down maple syrup. These are the jobs from which legends arise and associations begin: who hasn't heard of the archetypical Vermonter, as hard as marble on the outside and sweet as maple syrup inside?

Whether you are visiting a bustling workplace or a dormant factory, you will find yourself compelled to learn, admire and appreciate the diverse fruits of past and present labors.

SAUGUS IRON WORKS NATIONAL HISTORIC SITE

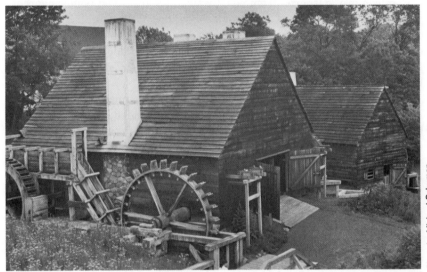

Long before Pittsburgh had even been settled, American colonists were forging iron on this spot in Saugus, Massachusetts.

QUICK. WHERE WAS THE AMERICAN STEEL INDUSTRY BORN?

Pittsburgh? Bethlehem, Pennsylvania? Bessemer, Alabama?

How about Saugus, Massachusetts?

Saugus it is. Only 21 years after the Pilgrims landed at Plymouth, the general court of Massachusetts Bay Colony put into effect an ordinance calling for the research, discovery and development of mineral deposits and other natural resources.

As migration from England dwindled after the 1630s, fewer iron products were imported, and the colonial government took keen interest in the untapped resources waiting to be discovered in this new world.

Thus by 1650, the first successful iron works was operating in this small town in the Massachusetts Bay Colony about 20 miles north of Boston.

In modern-day Saugus, tucked in the middle of a nondescript residential district, lies a fascinating reconstruction of this original iron works. A visit here is a trip to a part of colonial America usually ignored in most tourist destinations: early colonial industry. Here were the first steel workers in America.

Several buildings can be visited at Saugus Iron Works National Historic Site, a part of the national park system; three of them, however, were vital to the iron-making process: the furnace, the forge and the slitting mill.

Bog iron ore, gathered from nearby swampy areas and ponds; charcoal from acres of trees; and flux, a dark gabbro rock containing calcium carbonate that helps separate the iron from earthy parts of ore, were all dumped into the top of the furnace, the first building you see on your guided tour. The furnace was fired up, and within three days molten iron began to collect in the crucible.

Once or twice every 24 hours the furnace was tapped, and the molten iron ran into a furrow dug in the sand. Once hardened, the long cast iron bars—called "pigs" or "sows"—were ready to be taken to the forge for further refinement.

The forge was the busiest of the three buildings. In continual motion were four waterwheels and a great hammer pounding on the anvil. At the same time, three fires were raging, while the sinewy muscles of the workers were transforming the sows and pigs into malleable wrought iron bars which were then made into tools and structural materials.

The slitting mill, the last of the three buildings, was one of only about a dozen in the world at that time. It was used only when there were specific needs for flats, made by thrusting hot bars through sets of rollers and flattening them to proper lengths, or nail rods, made by reheating and passing them through cutting discs.

Even in the heat of summer, fires operate in this re-created iron works. So when you step into the forge and make your way close to the flames, you realize the degree of the heat in which laborers toiled. Their fires were going 12 hours a day, while today's are only at their hottest about five minutes per hour, but you will feel the discomfort they endured 330 years ago.

Many of the iron workers, you will hear on the guided tour and learn in the visitor center museum, hardly fell into the category of unskilled laborers. On the contrary, they were expert craftsmen recruited from iron-making regions of Great Britain. But, of course, somebody had to do the menial tasks, and the English brought over many Scottish prisoners of war as indentured workers to tackle the drudgery. (The park service states that in addition to the Scots, there were at least two Indians who were employed as unskilled workers.)

But even for the skilled craftsmen, the job was tough. Not only did they work in oppressive heat (the wheels shut down in the dead of winter when the Saugus River was frozen, cutting off waterpower needed to run the mills—although there was still plenty of other work to do), but they exposed themselves to ear-piercing noise, body-wrecking torturous labor (you will be amazed by the size and weight of the tools that were regularly used) and flying pieces of hot metal.

The majority of the workers, even those skilled in a craft, were un-educated; the majority could not read or write. As a rule, they were not religious and were frequently admonished for not attending church. A colonial Clint Eastwood might have confronted these "heavies." Brawls and drunken displays took place constantly, and, on any given day, you would likely see an ironworker in public court waiting to hear his pun-ishment for some offense.

While no diaries or letters have been left to clue in 20th-century his-torians on the personal lives of workers who became established colonists, there are records of marriages which show ironworkers and their sons and daughters married into local families, and hence ultimately accepted socially by the residents.

The iron works at Saugus didn't last long: the final recorded production here was in 1668, just 22 years after the first. You read in the visitors' center that the failure cannot be blamed on any one factor. One display explains, "Instead of drawing out bars of iron for the country's use, there was hammered out nothing but contention and lawsuits."

Mismanagement, high production costs, fixed prices and the inability to return a profit all led to the downfall of this very early industry. In short, Saugus was a classic case of a poorly managed business. But in the long run, the little iron works north of Boston was the foundation of the one-day-to-be-great iron and steel industries of the United States.

Location: Saugus Iron Works National Historic Site is at 244 Central Street in Saugus. From Interstate 95 (Route 128) take the Walnut Street exit for Saugus/Lynn and follow the signs toward Saugus. After crossing Route 1, follow the little brown signs to the iron works. **Admission** is free. **Hours:** The historic site is operated on a full scale in late spring, summer and early fall. It is open on a limited scale through the winter and early spring. **Allow** one and a half hours to see everything. **Infor-mation:** Saugus Iron Works National Historic Site, 244 Central Street, Saugus, MA 01906; (617) 233-0050. **Note:** You are offered the choice of walking through the iron works site on your own or taking the guided tour; we definitely advise you to take the tour. Once the tour is finished, you should plan to visit the blacksmith shop located beyond the slitting mill. Other options include a brief trip through the colonial iron works house or a self-guided walk along a nature trail on the property. Dress comfortably and wear good walking shoes; you'll spend much of your time outdoors here whether you take the tour or walk about on your own.

LOWELL NATIONAL HISTORICAL PARK AND SLATER MILL HISTORIC SITE

Hop on board this reproduced 1901 trolley as guide Terri Pollock takes you to the Lowell of long ago, a time when female employees earned $2.25 per 72-hour week.

Photo by Michael Schuman

THE MILL TOWNS OF NEW ENGLAND ARE RISING AGAIN AND NOWHERE is this more evident than in Lowell, Massachusetts, where the National Park Service and Massachusetts State Park system have combined to bring this former textile center back to the land of the living.

Further south, on a smaller scale, a private foundation has transformed Pawtucket, Rhode Island's, mill heritage into a lively 90-minute look at life and labor in 19th-century New England.

There was a time when saying to a friend, "Let's go to Lowell," would have been as eagerly received as asking, "How would you like to help me clean my bathtub?"

Well, things have changed!

Lowell is now one of the most stimulating and enjoyable places to spend leisure time. Just as Lowell was the setting for the start of the Industrial Revolution in the early 19th century, today it is the location of the first urban national park which pays tribute not to a single event or person, but to an entire period in history.

It might sound dry, but it isn't! When you visit Lowell National Historical Park, you take trolleys and boat rides, you listen to costumed interpreters in living-history presentations, you watch an entertaining and informative multi-image slide show, see and hear 88 operating power looms, visit a restored turbine, and explore an actual boarding house where Lowell's mill workers lived.

What you are absorbing is a story of people rather than dry facts.

Thomas Jefferson, for example: the third president and perhaps the greatest and most accomplished intellect in our country's history was disgusted by the squalid working conditions of industrial Europe, causing him to claim that America's future was in agriculture.

Francis Cabot Lowell: he believed fully in the concept of a planned industrial community; and when this idea was finally realized, the community took his name. Lowell—the man and not the city—conceived such idealized notions as a corporate structure, a work force of women, and company-maintained-and-supported living quarters.

Then there were the Boston Associates, a group of Francis Cabot Lowell's contemporaries, which was made up of the first investors in this dream community. And there was Kirk Boott, the powerful and forceful agent of the associates who helped make Francis Cabot Lowell's dream come true in the shape of buildings, canals, roads, and corporate policies.

Finally, the original list included the unskilled daughters of Yankee farmers, who became known throughout history as the "mill girls." They were the ones who initially took the jobs making textiles for a minimum wage of $2.25 per week, which usually consisted of 72 hours of work. The "mill girls" were later replaced by the immigrants from other countries who provided the labor needed to run the looms of "Spindle City."

To learn about these people and explore the park, you take either a guided tour of two and a half hours, or other shorter tours. The tours offer a combination of foot, trolley and boat transportation.

The trolleys are authentic reproductions of cars built in 1901 for the Boston and Northern Street Railway. They symbolize the social influence of the trolley. Some of you might even recall when a traveller could go from Atlantic City, New Jersey, to the state of Maine while using nothing but trolley transportation. The trolley also spawned the ancestors of today's suburbs, since mill workers no longer had to live across the street or around the corner from their place of employment.

The boats traverse canals built specifically for transportation and the flow of water which was integral to the distribution of power needed to keep the mills operating. The power source is the Merrimack River and this planned industrial community was built near the site of its powerful Pawtucket Falls. The canals were dug by the hands of immigrants. The locks in the canal system have recently been restored; for the first time since the turn of the century, boats can pass through them.

You will encounter living-history demonstrations on the tour. But the most impressive site might be the Boott Cotton Mills Museum, opened in 1992 in a mill complex over 150 years old. After your visit, you will probably recall the ear-assaulting din of 88 operating looms in the 1920s weave room. Imagine working in such a place. Better yet, listen to the remembrances of mill workers, whose oral histories are presented in a video presentation.

While the emphasis in Lowell is on the social impact of the Industrial Revolution as much as—or possibly more than—the technological achievements, Slater Mill Historic Site in Pawtucket, Rhode Island, focuses primarily on the magic of machinery invented and developed in the early 19th century.

While Lowell was the first planned industrial city, Pawtucket claims to be the "birthplace of American industry." The understandable reason for that grand title is clear; here, in 1793, English immigrant Samuel Slater and two Providence merchants, William Almy and Smith Brown, built the Old Slater Mill on the banks of the Blackstone River. This is where cotton yarn was first produced with water-powered machinery.

Slater Mill is still standing. A later structure, the Wilkinson Mill, built in 1810, is next door, also in its original location. The 1758 Sylvanus Brown House was moved here in the 1960s from a site elsewhere in Pawtucket.

The Sylvanus Brown House was the home of a millwright and patternmaker who worked for both the Slater and Wilkinson families. It is furnished according to Brown's probate inventory of 1824, showing us a typical household prior to the industrial revolution. Inside the Brown House are start-to-finish demonstrations of the manual production of cloth. Wool is first carded, then spun on a great wheel, and finally woven on a hand loom into cloth. In the basement, flax is processed into thread in a fashion common to the region.

After the natural wooden cord on the flax is broken on a flax breaker, the fibers are straightened as the flax is passed through a series of hatchels (boards spiked with nails) so that it may be spun on a Saxony wheel.

Courtesy: Slater Mill Historic Site

There is much to reflect upon when you visit the handsome but also very functional Slater Mill.

Yankee thrift was the rule; no waste was permitted. Flax left in hatchels or carders was woven into rags, towels, or twine.

At Slater Mill, you are entering the first world of machines. Samuel Slater, a man gifted with both good business and good mechanical sense, formed a partnership here in 1790; his first employees were seven boys and two girls ages seven to 12. Hiring youngsters was a common practice, since it was cheaper to hire children than high-priced adults.

Many of the 20-odd machines are still operative and are demonstrated in this mill building to illustrate the primary procedure in converting raw cotton to finished yarn. The line-up includes: a yarn-making throstle machine (built in Lowell in 1838, it is the oldest in the country that still works); a maypole braider, which made shoelaces; and a narrow fabric loom which was and still is used for making such articles as bookmarks. Slater Mill bookmarks are sold for a nominal charge in the gift shop.

While in this building, you learn about the seedy side of routine work in Samuel Slater's day. Disease ran rampant. Workers commonly sucked the ends of threads to pass them from one shuttle to another, and contagious illnesses like tuberculosis were commonly spread from one worker to the next. In a photograph on a wall inside the mill, you will see a group of male workers in a later period, the 1880s; even then, safety and health standards were abysmal. All the men in the picture have mustaches, and not because it was the fashion: mustaches were grown to be natural filters, keeping dust from getting in their mouths.

The final stop on the tour is the Wilkinson Mill built by Oziel Wilkinson; his son, David, was the American inventor of the industrial lathe. Inside the structure are lathes, sanders, drilling machines, and bobbin-making machines, demonstrating a working machine shop in the 19th century. When all the operative machines are running, the building is a whirring gaggle of belts and wheels, power being provided by an eight-ton water wheel underneath. The wheel was built in 1980, based on sketches of one used here in 1826. And yes, there is a link between the name of the falls on the Merrimack River in Lowell and the city where Slater Mill was built. "Pawtucket" was the name of a nomadic Indian tribe, part of the Penacook Confederacy, and the name means "place by the falls."

Location: Lowell National Historical Park. From Interstate 495, take the Lowell Connector towards Lowell and follow the signs. **Admission** is charged for tours. **Hours:** Year-round. **Allow** four hours to take main tour, see slide presentation, browse through visitor center, and visit the Boott Cotton Mills Museum; less time for shorter tours, slide presentation and visitor center. **Information:** Lowell National Historical Park, 169 Merrimack Street, Lowell, MA 01852; (508) 970-5000. **Note:** Reservations are suggested. If you have visited Lowell or have a specific interest, consider taking one of the many tours devoted to single topics: mill girls, water power, Lowell history, tunes and tales of the mill era and immigrants.

Location: Slater Mill Historic Site. Northbound Interstate 95, take exit 28, turn left from exit and head straight; turn right onto Roosevelt Avenue to site. Southbound Interstate 95, take exit 29, turn right onto Fountain Street and right onto Exchange Street; then turn left onto Roosevelt Avenue to site. **Admission** is charged. **Hours:** June through Labor Day, Tuesday through Sunday; weekends March through May, Labor Day through mid-December. **Allow** an hour and a half for the complete tour. **Information:** Slater Mill Historic Site, P.O. Box 727, Pawtucket, RI 02862; (401) 725-8638. **Note:** Buy tickets in the gift shop before joining tour.

NEW ENGLAND MAPLE MUSEUM AND NEW ENGLAND SUGAR HOUSES

Photo by Michael Schuman

Peter Barrett working at the evaporator at Barrett's Sugar House in Keene, New Hampshire.

TRY EXPLAINING TO A NON-NEW ENGLANDER THAT HE OR SHE MIGHT enjoy eating fresh snow. In response, you will get some funny looks and perhaps a few disparaging comments.

But if you mention that the snow will be topped with a maple-flavored, taffy-textured delicacy, and that it is a traditional northern New England treat, you will likely get a more inquisitive, if not affirmative, answer. Offer a few samples and you will be barraged with requests for more.

Indulging in sugar on snow is the benefit reserved for those who trek up to the north country during sugaring season, usually mid-March to mid-April, when the farmers are hard at work boiling sap down. A day trip to this region allows you to visit sugar houses and a museum explaining the history of this sweet staple.

The legend goes like this: a few centuries ago, an Iroquois squaw went out after a rainstorm to gather rainwater for cooking. She found some beneath the broken limb of a maple tree, and upon cooking with it, noticed an unusually sweet aroma and taste that her main course had unsuspectingly acquired. And so, the maple sugaring industry in Vermont was born.

The New England Maple Museum in Pittsford, Vermont—just north of Rutland—portrays this legend in a mural and with centuries-old wooden troughs that were actually used by New England Indians for catching maple sap. The museum, recently expanded, is designed with a time line effect, starting with these crude troughs. Accompanying the exhibits is a series of murals painted exclusively for the museum; each depicts some period in the development of the sugaring industry in Vermont.

As you progress, you see more recent sugaring utensils; the troughs give way to wooden buckets, then galvanized steel buckets and the modern plastic tubing used so commonly today. In addition to the varied receptacles used for sap-catching, there are many other antiques: a rustic ox cart, an ox-drawn wooden sap sled, tin maple molds, and a cast iron kettle.

This presentation of sugaring history is capped by a simulated display of tubing drawing sap from a tree as well as a 10-minute slide show. Narrated by NBC News's Peter Hackes, it focuses on the sugaring operation of a Vermont family which still uses hand power—shunning modern conveniences like gasoline- or battery-powered tappers—to pound taps into their trees.

All those questions that pop into your head while driving past bucket- and tube-laden maple trees in late winter and early spring are answered. Does it matter how old or how tall the trees are? How many buckets of sap are needed to make one gallon of syrup? Are there any states outside New England that produce large quantities of maple products? The explanations are all here, and you might be surprised by a few of them. For example, the area around Pittsburgh, Pennsylvania, is known by locals for its syrup as much as its steel.

The building housing the museum was built from scratch by Vermonters Tom and Dona Olson and was designed to look like a 19th-century sugarhouse. Although it is a reproduction, it is just about the only thing relating to Vermont maple syrup here which is not the real thing.

If you are in northern New England during sugaring season, you will find many sugar houses giving tours of their facilities and selling sweet maple treats. We are limiting the following list mainly to those sugar houses located in the quiet Monadnock Region of southwestern New Hampshire. To find others, just track down that wispy circle of smoke rising above the bare woods in March or April.

Bacon's Sugar House, Jaffrey Center, New Hampshire. You can tour a grove of maple trees, commonly referred to as a sugarbush (although Charlie Bacon says real New Englanders don't use that term when referring to such a grove), while the boiling down is taking place. Bacon's offers sugar parties on weekends which, in addition to the sugarbush tour, include a visit inside a sugar house and samples of sugar on snow for sale. **Information:** (603) 532-8836.

Barrett's Sugar House, Keene, New Hampshire. This former schoolhouse offers no formal tours, but you can visit and chat with workers. Early afternoons on weekends are the best times to catch the sap boiling. Free syrup samples are offered to visitors. **Information:** (603) 352-6812.

Bascom's Sugar House, Alstead, New Hampshire. On weekends, 15-minute-long tours are offered. Sugar on snow (complete with the pickle to offset the sweetness) is sold as are doughboys (fried bread dough) with syrup and maple pecan pie. **Information:** (603) 835-2230 or 835-6361.

Clark's Sugar House, Alstead, New Hampshire. Five generations of Clarks have been producing maple syrup here since 1910. Tours are given on weekends; weekday tours are by appointment. Wooden buckets, handmade sap yokes, tanks and sap spouts are part of a permanent display of antique equipment. Sugar on snow, maple pecan pie, coffee and doughnuts are for sale. **Information:** (603) 835-6863.

Harlow's Sugar House, Putney, Vermont. We cross the state line for this perennial favorite. Horse-drawn wagon or, depending on snow cover, sleigh rides have been offered in the past; Harlow's is considering giving them once more, but call ahead first. There is a short film, and an explanation of sugaring is given as you watch the sap boiling. Goodies available include sugar on snow, corn fritters with syrup, coffee, and doughnuts. **Information:** (802) 387-5852.

Putnam Brothers Sugar House, Charlestown, New Hampshire. Come by on a weekend any time during sugaring season and you will have your choice of sugar on snow, or doughnuts and coffee. Tours are offered. **Information:** (603) 826-3296 or 826-5515.

Stuart and John's Sugar House, Westmoreland, New Hampshire. A restaurant where maple delicacies are served accompanies the sugar house here. You can see boiling in progress on weekends. **Information:** (603) 399-4486.

Note: We strongly recommend that you call first before visiting any sugar houses. Sugaring season varies greatly depending on the weather and its beginning and end can differ by weeks from the previous year. Also, keep in mind that all these listed are family-run and can change their operations from one season to the next.

Location: The New England Maple Museum is on Route 7 north of Rutland, Vermont. **Admission** is charged. **Hours:** Daily, mid-March through late December. **Allow** 45 minutes. **Information:** New England Maple Museum, P.O. Box 1615, Rutland, VT 05701; (802) 483-9414. **Note:** The opening and closing dates for the museum are variable; in March or after Columbus Day, call first before making a special trip to see the museum.

CANTERBURY SHAKER VILLAGE

Officially they were called the United Society of Believers in Christ's Second Coming, but most of us have always been fascinated by the people we call the Shakers. Here, a group poses at the Canterbury Shaker Village trustees office.

WE STOOD INSIDE THE BROAD MEETING HOUSE STARING AT THE BLUE ceiling that hadn't been painted for 111 years. It looked as if someone had applied a coat just last week.

"The Shakers knew nothing about planned obsolescence," said Charles (Bud) Thompson, curator, tour guide, non-Shaker and resident of Canterbury Shaker Village, Canterbury, New Hampshire.

"People from a paint manufacturing company came here to look at this ceiling. They wanted to make sure they would never put in their paint what's in this paint."

When you think of early American communal or Utopian communities, the Amish of Pennsylvania and the Midwest, the Oneidas of upstate New York, the Amanas of eastern Iowa and, of course, the Shakers (who earned their nickname from the quaking motions they practiced while praying—some outsiders erroneously called them Shaking Quakers) come to mind.

It is ironic: the Shaker religion, once so healthy, is on the verge of extinction, while the Shakers are more admired and respected than ever before. A peace-loving, hard-working people, the Shakers' inventiveness and practical creativity still influence our lives.

The Shakers are credited with the invention of the flat broom, the clothespin, and the slat back chair. Shaker-style crafts are in great demand. Many who live in the West and Midwest are so intrigued by the Shakers' ideals and life patterns that they put one of the Northeast's Shaker villages on their cross-country itineraries.

During the tour you will be led through five village buildings left virtually as they were when the community was thriving. At one point in the mid-19th century, there were more than 250 residents; the last Shaker Sister died in 1992.

Why is the Shaker religion dying? You will hear the explanation here. Mother Ann Lee, an Englishwoman, brought eight followers to America in 1774 and settled the first Shaker community. These disciples felt that Jesus's second coming had occurred and the Messiah had taken the form of Mother Ann. Despite the fact that they were led by a woman, certainly a handicap then, and that they had come from England in the year before the first skirmish of the American Revolution, the Shakers grew. By 1850, they claimed 6,000 members in 18 villages stretching from New England to Kentucky.

The nine cardinal principles of the Shaker religion, officially called the United Society of Believers in Christ's Second Coming, included honesty, kindness, diligence, prudence, education and purity. The last principle was the most controversial. Although it would seem that the Shakers' decline was due to their adherence to a celibate lifestyle, Shaker Village curator Bud Thompson asked us to consider other possibilities.

As we stood between the meeting house and what was once expansive garden land, Thompson noted that it was the Shakers' stringent belief in quality production that led to their demise.

The Industrial Revolution flooded the market with inferior products, said Thompson, and the Shakers wouldn't compromise their values. They couldn't compete with rapid production of cheaper items and, in a reversal of American economic trends, became more reliant on agriculture than industry.

The Shakers gained new members through adoption and voluntary conversion. However, a law went into effect which forbade adoption of children by religious groups unless the children were born into that religion. Shaker adoptees were allowed to leave the community upon their 21st birthday, but the law severely curtailed membership.

The remnants of this once active community are seen on the tour.

In the meeting house, the building which boasts the 111-year-old paint job, you see parades of pegs jutting out from the walls. With orderliness a predominant rule, everything from tools to furniture was hung on pegs.

Typical Shaker inventions include a pin cushion with a vise-like base, making it easily moved from one table to the next, and the flat broom. You'll hear that the Shakers were the first people to raise, package, and sell garden seeds commercially.

They also led the way in utilizing the concept of built-in furniture, as exemplified in the home of Elder Henry Blinn, whom Bud Thompson recalled as a man whose generosity flowed like the Connecticut River during the April thaw. Throughout Blinn's house are built-in drawers and closets, making very efficient use of space.

Unlike the Amish, the Shakers welcomed electricity; in the community laundry room, the gargantuan machines there were first operated by steam power, then by electricity.

Also unlike the Amish, the Shakers had no aversion to colorful clothing. Their tastes were simple, but not bland; dark red, blue and light green prints supplement the grey, white and black garments displayed.

The Shaker knack for precision and invention is explained in the Shaker schoolhouse. Mathematics was emphasized, and children learned to do their multiplication tables and additions quickly. When you walk into the first floor in this room, you are actually entering the second floor. An additional story was needed many years ago, and the villagers built it by raising the entire building and putting the new floor underneath the original. The roof is the same one that has been there since the schoolhouse was first constructed.

Why didn't the Shakers expand and take in new members? According to Thompson, the Shaker community was always a dual society, governed by both men and women. Some years ago, the three then surviving Shakers at Canterbury, all women, decided that since there were no men to help lead, they would not attempt to keep the community growing. Here, then, is literally the last of an era.

Location: From Interstate 93, exit 18, head east through Canterbury, following the signs for the village. **Admission** is charged. **Hours:** May through October, daily; weekends in April, November, and December. **Allow** an hour and a half for the tour. **Information:** Canterbury Shaker Village, Canterbury, NH 03224; (603) 783-9511. **Note:** Your time on the tour is spent evenly outdoors and indoors so dress for the weather. You also might consider spending time in the gift shop, where fine quality Shaker reproductions are for sale.

WESTERN GATEWAY HERITAGE STATE PARK AND OTHER MASSACHUSETTS HERITAGE STATE PARKS

Courtesy: Western Gateway Heritage State Park

In its day, the construction of the Hoosac Tunnel brought prosperity to North Adams, Massachusetts. Today, the tunnel is doing the same as its story of sweat and toil is being told in the visitor center at Western Gateway Heritage State Park.

NORTH ADAMS, MASSACHUSETTS WAS NEVER MEANT TO BE A TOURIST attraction. Neither were small Bay State cities such as Lawrence, Lynn, Gardner, and Holyoke. They were seats of sweat, the industrial backbone of an industrial state.

The Commonwealth of Massachusetts has revitalized these cities in the Massachusetts Urban Heritage State Park program, in which museums, interpretive programs, walking tours, shops and restaurants are bringing people into these cities for pleasure as opposed to work. Because of this, these former centers of manufacturing are once again important cogs in the economy of the state.

Historically North Adams was one of the cities most vital to the fiscal health of 19th-century Massachusetts. When the Hoosac Tunnel was completed in 1875, the big cities of the eastern end of the state had a clear path to the expanding West. By 1895, 60 percent of Boston's trade arrived by way of the tunnel. With good reason, the citizens of North Adams boasted: "We hold the western gateway."

Appropriately, the name Western Gateway Heritage State Park has been given to the refurbished section of historic North Adams, opened to the public in October 1985.

It is also fitting that the location of this tribute to tedious toil, brain power, and the might of the locomotive is the North Adams freight yard, officially known as the National Register of Historic Places District. Here, an even half dozen warehouses dating from the turn of the century have been converted into specialty shops, a restaurant, and a Visitors' Center which has a permanent exhibit devoted to the industries and the engineering feats which made this area of the state prosper. First and foremost was the Hoosac Tunnel.

In its day, it was the largest railroad tunnel in the world, measuring 4.75 miles. The large exhibit devoted to the Hoosac Tunnel is itself placed inside a simulated tunnel in the visitor center. Enter it and hear the sound of nitroglycerin exploding, followed instantly by a flash of light.

Walk a little further and you can read about the exploits that made possible this marvel of mankind's determination. The men worked with few tools, mainly some sighting transits and plumb bobs. When workers at each end of the tunnel finally met each other, the total error in alignment was less than one inch in 25,000 feet!

But not everybody wanted the Hoosac Tunnel to be built. A hypothetical debate between two 19th-century politicians is heard as you progress deeper into the exhibit. One who favors the project stresses how the tunnel will open up Boston and eastern Massachusetts to the growing inland market. You hear that many opponents were motivated by their own interests, especially those who had invested heavily in the Boston & Worcester and the Western Railroad; they felt that the tunnel would lower freight rates, thereby reducing the values of their investments.

Others opposed worried about the money needed to complete the formidable job; after all, the price tag was exorbitant: $20,000,000. But there was a more significant cost, that of human lives. A total of 196 men perished in the construction of the Hoosac Tunnel.

Many of those who worked on the body-wrenching project to its completion, predominantly Irish and French-Canadian immigrants, stayed in North Adams to work its mills. Other immigrants eventually came from far-reaching ports: there were the Welsh, the Italians, the Cornish, and even some Chinese who settled in the community as shoe workers.

Most of them also worked in mills, making fabrics, machinery, and wood and stone products. Until the advent of the trolley, most lived within walking distance of their jobs; inevitably, a profusion of small businesses and trades such as tinsmiths, blacksmiths, masons, and teamsters grew alongside the mill complexes. In spite of the relatively large revenue the railroad brought in, North Adams became more than just an eastern railroad town. Through old photographs, murals, and written commentary, you discover other claims to North Adams's fame. Who remembers that North Adams was a hot air ballooning center at the turn of the century?

But the main thrust of the Visitors' Center at Western Gateway Heritage State Park is the railroad. Check your weight on an original freight scale, touch rocks that were once parts of the mountain where the Hoosac Tunnel is now, and watch one of many films exploring the world of rails.

Other Massachusetts Heritage State Parks are:

Lowell Heritage State Park: run in conjunction with Lowell National Historical Park, this is the granddaddy of all urban state and national parks. Through trolley rides, boat rides, and ranger-led walks into gatehouses and mills, visitors gain an understanding of the once-thriving textile industry and the Industrial Revolution of which it was part. (508) 453-1950.

Lawrence Heritage State Park: another look at the textile industry; this park offers historical exhibits, summer concerts, an art gallery, and a visitor center in a restored workers' boarding house. (508) 685-2591 for recorded information on activities, (508) 794-1655 for additional information.

Lynn Heritage State Park: the Lynn waterfront has been restored with specialty shops, restaurants and a marina. There are exhibits focusing on Lynn's industrial past with emphasis on shoemaking and the General Electric Company. Harbor tours are offered. (617) 598-1974.

Heritage State Park at Battleship Cove in Fall River: here, the visitor center offers a multi-slide presentation of Fall River's textile industry. At its peak, this waterside city produced more cloth than any other city in the nation. Refurbished mill buildings house factory outlets, and Battleship Cove offers tours of a battleship, a destroyer, a submarine, and the Marine Museum. (508) 675-5759.

Holyoke Heritage State Park: by hopping on an antique rail car, you can take a tour of both this industrial city and the surrounding countryside. Mill buildings house outlets and restaurants, and the visitor center's exhibits summarize Holyoke's history. Also on the grounds are a children's museum and the Volleyball Hall of Fame. (413) 534-1723.

Gardner Heritage State Park: a historic firehouse is home for the visitor center, which incorporates hands-on exhibits and interpretive displays to showcase Gardner's furniture industry. Just outside downtown is Dunn Pond where picnicking is available. (508) 630-1497 or (508) 632-2099 for a recorded message.

Location: Western Gateway Heritage State Park is at the junction of Routes 2 and 8 in North Adams. **Admission** is free. **Hours:** Year-round; daily, Memorial Day through October; closed Tuesday and Wednesday the rest of the year. **Allow** 45 minutes to tour the visitor center, more to shop or dine. **Information:** Western Gateway Heritage State Park, 9 Furnace Street Bypass, North Adams, MA 01247; (413) 663-6312 or (413) 663-8059 for a recorded message. **Note:** Gift boutiques, craft shops and restaurants are also in the Heritage State Park complex.

MAINE MARITIME MUSEUM

"How much a pound?" Whatever the going rate when you visit the Maine Maritime Museum, you'll learn that the lobsterman works hard for his money.

"HOW MUCH A POUND?"

So asks the life-sized model of a lobsterman through a prerecorded cassette tape in the Maine Maritime Museum in Bath.

"That's what you want to know. How much a pound?"

As we watch and listen to him talk about his job, we absorb his surroundings. He stands in a shed boxed-in by lobster pots—some finished, some just being crafted. His well-worn jacket hangs on a peg on the back wall along with a virtual hardware store of tools. He holds a paint brush in one hand and a blue can that formerly contained one of America's favorite coffees in the other. Around him are buoys and bundles of rope, and on a wall in his shed is a sign that once graced the front desk of another larger establishment; it says, "Street girls bringing sailors into hotel must pay for room in advance."

The lobsterman continued to talk about his trade—the hard work, the rough seas, the long hours. But he is still not ready to answer, "How much a pound?"

His great-grandfather, he is happy to let us know, sold lobsters for two cents a pound. Around 1916, his grandfather told him he got a dime per pound. In the 1950s a going price was 34 cents a pound, and in the mid 1970s, a fair deal would have brought in $2.20 for sixteen ounces of lobster meat.

Finally, we hear, "How much a pound?" once more. The lobsterman tosses the query right back to us, asking what we would want to be paid if we had to do his work.

Some visitors laugh at that answer. Some sneer. But the point is well-taken.

Lobstering sounds romantic to many. A life at sea would sure beat office routine and a business suit.

But when we learn that lobstermen work from six to twelve hours a day up to seven days a week, all the executives with fancy cars in the museum parking lot, and all the teachers pausing here on their annual 12-week summer vacations stop feeling sorry for themselves.

And when visitors sit in the re-created lobster boat named the *Linda J* to watch an 18-minute videotape on the loneliness and monotony that fills a lobsterman's day, suddenly the free and adventurous life seems decidedly less appealing. (Bear in mind that the videotape was made for the television program "Omnibus" in 1954. Though it still captures the essence of the work, lobstermen earn considerably more money now than when the tape was made. The subject of the presentation, Eugene Eaton, is well into his sixties and still lobstering off the Maine coast.)

Exposure to work done on and around the sea is the *raison d'être* of the Maine Maritime Museum, which sits on the shores of the Kennebec River on the former site of the Percy and Small shipyard.

In this multi-building museum, tribute is paid to every ocean-bound or seaside way of earning a living. Boat building, battle fighting, fishing and trading are a few of the other occupations portrayed.

Lobsters, being synonymous with the state of Maine, are a main interest of most visitors, and the lobster exhibit, paid for in part by L.L. Bean, Inc., could stand as a museum in itself.

Listening to the recorded talk of the lobsterman and watching the videotape will occupy only part of your time. Stroll through and learn more. What were lobstermen's most common superstitions? For starters, they never painted their boats blue or uttered the word "pig" while aboard.

If you have ever wondered how those lobster pots that seem so photogenic piled by the water's edge actually work, this is the place to learn. Lobsters are lured into the caged box's first chamber (called the "kitchen") with a bag of bait. Then, while trying to escape, they are misled by the pot's funnel-shaped entrance and chamber into the second chamber (the "parlor"). There, a trap vent for undersized lobsters and other small animals permits the pip-squeaks to escape.

Perhaps the lobster's best ticket to immortality is the Maine gift shop (it often seems there is one for every grain of sand on the Maine shoreline). Before leaving the lobster exhibit, stop for a peek at the collection of lobster-adorned trinkets: key chains, pencils, tee shirts, spoon rests. There's an inflatable lobster, and a bumper sticker that reads, "To hell with the beef. Where's the lobster?"

You will probably spend most of your time in the lobstering exhibit. But don't overlook the others, which afford an important glimpse of sea-farers' ways.

The Percy and Small shipyard is the only one in the country still intact. This is where the wooden sailing behemoths so common in bygone decades were crafted and built. Captain Samuel R. Percy, a Republican and son of a captain from Phippsburg, Maine, and Frank Small, a Bath Democrat and also the son of a captain, started building boats here in 1897 and continued through 1920, constructing 41 four-, five- and six-masted schooners, including the *Wyoming*, the largest wooden sailing vessel ever to take to the sea from the United States.

Five of the original Percy and Small buildings are still standing, one of which, the Mill and Joiner Shop, was built with awning doors which, when opened, swung upward to allow for long timbers to be brought inside; here, the timbers were cut and carved to form fancy cabin interiors.

To see hands in action on restoration projects, climb to the second floor of the small craft center. An apprenticeship program was started by the Maine Maritime Museum in 1972; since then, newcomers to the ship crafting industry have donated their labor in return for the opportunity to learn from the experts. You are welcome to watch them at work and to ask questions. While inside, note the collection of small craft on the first floor.

For years, the museum's holdings included the contents of two additional buildings further up Washington Street. But in June, 1989, it was all moved into a brand new structure, the Maritime History Building; it is there that you will discover more about life at sea.

The principal exhibition, "A Maritime History of Maine," describes the many ways that the state's seafarers have faced the challenges of their profession. Beginning with early exploration and the unsuccessful Popham Colony of 1607–08, Maine's maritime heritage is told in a series of exhibit areas focusing on: early settlement, fishing, local and world trade, shipbuilding in wood and steel, ships and war, coastal transportation, and pleasure boating.

Be nosy and peek inside a 19th century seaman's chest to see what he might have taken on board ship. Take a look at his sleeping quarters in a reconstruction of the forecastle of a 19th century ship. Or, look at the tools our hypothetical sailor would have taken with him: speaking trumpets (like Rudy Vallee's old megaphone), foghorns, log glasses, sextants, an English leather bound telescope, and an assortment of time pieces and compasses.

Upon returning to his home port, the travel-weary sailor would have presented his wife or parents with treasures from all parts of the world, like the bamboo from the Seychelles Islands or the alabaster Buddha from India, that are likely to be on view when you visit.

There is also a display area for ship models and maritime art. Note the *Northampton*, described as a "classic ship portrait" with its detail and lack of drama, in contrast to the *Servia*, with its active crew. You will also find newly exhibited works by ship-portrait artists Antonio Jacobsen and S.F.M. Badger.

Just up the road is the Bath Iron Works, a century old and still an important, active shipyard. Large windows in the museum building will let visitors have a first-hand look at the busy boat-building plant. When we last visited, two new Navy cruisers were almost ready for launching while a third was covered with scaffolding, about half finished.

If you have your children in hand, make a point of stopping at the children's play area by the waterfront. If you are lucky, you may get to see the 142-foot Grand Banks fishing schooner *Sherman Zwicker*—if it's in port.

Location: From Interstate 95, take the exit for Route 1 (Brunswick-Bath Coastal Route); take the Washington Street exit in Bath and turn right for the museum at 243 Washington. **Admission** is charged. **Hours:** Year-round, daily. **Allow** at least a half day, up to a full day to see the entire museum. **Information:** Maine Maritime Museum, 243 Washington Street, Bath, ME 04530; (207) 443-1316. **Note:** Picnic tables are on the grounds and light lunches are available in summer. As with many museums, there is more in the collection than there is room to display, so exhibits may change. Also, there is one new gallery set aside specifically for changing exhibits.

THE BILLINGS FARM AND MUSEUM

Photo by Michael Schuman

There was plenty to do around a 19th-century New England farm even during the winter, as this ice-cutting exhibit at Billings Farm and Museum demonstrates.

A FARMER'S WIFE NAMED MRS. WILLIAMSON WHO RESIDED IN HARTland, Vermont about 100 years ago wrote the following about one typical morning's work:

"Made a fire, mended pants, set breakfast going, skimmed ten pans of milk, washed the pans, ate breakfast, went to the barn and milked two cows, brought the cream out of the cellar, churned 15 pounds of butter, made four apple pies, two mince pies and one custard pie, done up the sink. All done by nine o'clock."

And we really think we are something when we jog two miles and get to work five minutes early!

People have chosen farming for different reasons, but few have become farmers because the work was easy and the hours were short. After a visit to the Billings Farm and Museum in Woodstock, Vermont, you leave with an appreciation of farm labor and life, both then and now.

An unusual attraction among New England's many sites, the Billings Farm is both a working commercial dairy and a museum depicting Vermont farm life in the 1890s. The farm has been operating continuously since Woodstock lawyer, railroad executive, and philanthropist Frederick Billings established it in 1871. Not one to settle for second best, he stocked it with prize Jersey cattle imported directly from the Isle of Jersey in England. The museum was opened in 1983 by Laurance S. Rockefeller, as, in a sense, a living memorial to Billings, Mrs. Rockefeller's grandfather.

The tour reminds us that farming, difficult in general, is twice as tough in Vermont. The hillsides are stony, the land is not rich, and the season is short, with cold weather for up to eight months. (We don't have to tell you that, do we?)

After watching a stimulating introductory slide show, the first exhibit you see is called "Making the Land Produce." Small tools and large farm implements—and just about everything you see here is authentic—convey farming basics in the Green Mountain State.

These farmer's helpers rest in quiet retirement; they include: a grubbing plow, a crowbar, threshing machines, pitchforks and a grain cradle, which is an early scythe with outstretched prongs like five fingers. You walk past gear for four-legged creatures, including ox yokes and muzzles. The farmer's favorite Morgan has a blanket to prevent chilling, a lace cap to discourage flies, and a nosebasket for lunch time.

Enhancing the bigger exhibits are clear and concise commentaries explaining procedures, customs and traditions of farm life a century ago. For example, a red-patterned tablecloth is sprawled across a simulated field. On it are plates, pitchers, jars, baskets, and an appetizing loaf of bread. The tradition it illustrates was called "nooning," named for the time, appropriately enough, when lunch was eaten outdoors while work was in progress.

It wasn't often that such a lavish picnic could be accommodated within a farmer's busy schedule. Since the farmer was always in a hurry to make the best use of every available minute of sunshine, he usually gobbled down food and immediately returned to work. But occasionally there was an opportunity for a more festive meal—the likes of which are displayed—prior to returning to work in the fields.

In the torrid summer sun, haying was hot and tiring, often taking its toll on farm laborers. Pitching hay in the hot, musty loft of a barn was additional drudgery. To revive themselves and relieve their thirst, farmers and their hands drank switchel, a sort of 19th-century version of Gatorade. Switchel was a beverage made from spring water, molasses, ginger, vinegar, and often a handful of raw oatmeal; oatmeal was thought to help prevent heat prostration.

Then there were those tedious chores that extended well beyond the planting season. Said one farmer, "The great thing about firewood is that it warms you twice, once when you cut it and again when you burn it."

The display on firewood is sandwiched between those portraying the building of stone walls and re-creating a typical farm workshop. The assemblage of wood-splitting tools—a splitting ax, a sledge hammer and some wedges—looks familiar.

Antique butter molds and cheese hoops help illustrate the dairy farming displays, and the highlight here is the milk wagon used by Calvin Coolidge's grandfather to carry milk to his family's cheese factory.

The Vermont farmer's routines extended far beyond the walls of the barn and the borders of the fields. You visit his home, traditionally a woman's domain, where mannekins add a personalizing touch to a re-created two-story 19th-century farm house—with its front walls cut away and with its interior exposed.

In the kitchen, a woman tastes the evening meal which is cooking in a pot on the stove, a hearty stew perhaps; her daughter stands at a rough-hewn wooden table and flattens dough with a rolling pin. A cradle holding a tired baby rocks gently in the foreground, and a hand pump sits starkly by a wooden sink.

The informal parlor is realistically decorated with early American stencilling; many farm families left such wall art unchanged over a period of several generations.

The significance of the church, the school, and the town hall in a rural community is depicted in modest settings. The general store, on the other hand, looks complete and authentic, well-supplied with everything from Victorian postcards to a barrel with a checkerboard on top, the perfect setting for two oldsters to take out the checkers and start playing. Square tin containers and round cans are crammed on shelves behind the main counter, and a sign in the front window urges all to "Keep Your Pants On with the Atwood Suspender."

Sugaring and ice-cutting exhibits wind up the tour; the latter process is especially interesting, showing how blocks of ice are sawed out of frozen lakes and ponds and transferred to storage for later use—a chore that was still being done in remoter rural areas in the 1940s.

Near the exhibits' entrance and exit is a small gift and book shop, where carefully selected books about farming can be purchased.

From the museum a fenced path leads to the Billings Dairy, where the details of managing a blue-ribbon herd of Jerseys are explained. For instance, calves are given three names, with the first indicating the breeder, the second the sire, and the third is the calf's own name: "Vaucluse Empire Suzette" was bred by the Vaucluse Farm with a sire named Empire. All the members of her immediate family have names beginning with the letters "Su"; Suzette's grandmother was Susan, her mother was Suzanne, her sister is Suette and her daughters and granddaughters have names like Sue Ann, Sue Ellen, Suella and Sulinda. (Don't ask whether the cows know the difference.)

Entering the dairy barns, we saw cows as well as sprightly calves just born. Milking takes place daily at 5:30 A.M. and 3:30 P.M. If you are around in the afternoon, you can see milk flowing through clear tubing, above your heads, from vacuum operated mechanical milkers. Staff personnel are on hand to answer your questions.

In 1989, the 1890 farm house was restored and opened as part of the farm tour. The rambling Victorian house was the centerpiece of this progressive farm and was the home of farm manager George Aitken, a mustached Scottish immigrant who, when not taking care of the farm's business, was partial to big game hunting. The mounted bear claws and deer head in his office are evidence of this pastime.

The office is a dark, panelled room with portraits of farm cows of the day—all Jerseys—covering the walls. Though ornate wood stoves kept the living quarters warm, George and Margaret Aitken and their four daughters probably never felt totally at home here—thanks to the noises and odors emanating from the creamery one flight down. Also part of the building was the ice house with its cold-storage room, which along with the creamery, were reminders that this building's purpose was to serve as the farm's central processing facility as well as the Aitkens' residence.

Location: Billings Farm and Museum is on River Road in Woodstock. Take Interstate 91 to Interstate 89 north in White River Junction, Vermont. Take exit 1 (Route 4) and follow Route 4 to Route 12 in Woodstock (Elm Street). Cross the Elm Street bridge and continue for one half mile until you see signs for the farm and museum. **Admission** is charged. **Hours:** May through October, daily; weekends in November and December. **Allow** two hours to two and a half hours. **Information:** Billings Farm and Museum, River Road, P.O. Box 489, Woodstock, VT 05091; (802) 457-2355.

ROCK OF AGES GRANITE QUARRY

It takes body-wrenching labor to break off a piece of the earth.

THE QUARRY SHUTTLE PULLED US TOWARDS OUR DESTINATION—THE E.L. Smith Quarry, at Rock of Ages near Barre, Vermont.

The piles of granite chunks we passed resembled television news footage of the aftermath of a great earthquake: Rubble piled upon rubble. We supposed that this granite was being saved for use some months or years later.

"No way," we were told by our guide. These piles were just scrap. Junk. The term used in the granite business is grout, a Scottish word for waste.

She let us know that more than two thirds of the granite quarried is tossed aside because of streaks, spots or other imperfections. The finished products, as varied as graveside memorials or chess tables—some of which are displayed in the Rock of Ages Visitors' Center—are derived from only the balance of the granite actually quarried.

You appreciate the dangers inherent in working in a place like Rock of Ages when you reach the edge of the E.L. Smith quarry and peer down inside the mammoth, 50-acre cavity. All the hazards of working here are not immediately apparent; you are too high up to experience the noise, the climate inside the quarry, and the muscle-wracking labor expended.

Our guide told us that the noise inside the quarry is deafening to the point that earplugs, earmuffs or some other form of protection is a must. Verbal conversation is impossible; workers inside the quarry communicate by means of hand signals. Strident whistles located at different parts of the quarry warn workers when blocks are about to be moved.

"It is 10–20 degrees cooler in the quarry than it is up here," she said. "The quarries are operated nine or ten months a year, and the men stay warm by taking breaks inside heated aluminum huts."

Work ceases, she added, in certain situations, such as on those days when winter rain or snow turns to sleet and makes the rock piles too slippery.

Inside the quarry, you can see what appears to be a giant's game of Pick Up Sticks. All the huge spars and the ladders near them have important purposes. All the granite removed from the quarry is lifted by hoists that power the derricks. The derricks lower workers to their stations while the ladders serve as an emergency way out in case of a power failure.

How high are the derricks? You find out on the tour. But here's a hint; they were made from Oregon fir trees and shipped to Vermont on the backs of three flat cars each.

You also see yellow steel derricks. These are slowly taking the place of the wooden ones as age catches up with them.

As we returned to the Visitors' Center, our guide answered questions commonly asked by visitors. How long can the earth keep supplying granite? Geologists say we will run out in the year 3210. What is the difference between granite and marble? Marble is a metamorphic rock, granite is igneous. Marble is mined and granite is quarried. Marble is less durable and easier to carve than granite.

We hopped off the shuttle and walked to a nearby observation deck, where we gazed into Rock of Ages Quarry, an elephantine 350-foot-deep hole quarried for over a century. On our way back, we noticed Hercules, a saddle-tank locomotive that hauled cargo for both the Barre and Chelsea Railroad and the Rock of Ages Quarry; it rests in retirement as a diversion and a conversation piece.

Two models—a scale one of the E.L. Smith Quarry and an artificial human one garbed in quarry workers' protective equipment (goggles, ear muffs, safety belts, respirators, a rain suit, safety shoes and red gloves——draw your attention in the Visitors' Center.

A mile away is the Manufacturing Division. We walked across its observation platform, first overwhelmed by the scope of this cavernous building, then mesmerized by the workers' patience and skill in turning raw granite into refined finished products.

Location: Rock of Ages Granite Quarry is in Graniteville, Vermont, near Barre. From Interstate 89, take exit 6 and follow the signs to the quarry, about seven miles away. **Admission** is charged for the shuttle. It is free to the Visitors' Center and Manufacturing Division. **Hours:** May through October, daily, for the Visitors' Center; and Monday through Friday June through mid-October for the shuttle ride and Manufacturing Division. **Allow** an hour and a half to two hours to see everything and take the shuttle tour. **Information:** Rock of Ages Granite Quarry, P.O. Box 482, Barre, VT 05641; (802) 476-3119. **Note:** Picnic tables are near the Visitors' Center. You can bring your own picnic or buy ready-made sandwiches in the sugar house at the site. There is a souvenir shop in the Visitors' Center, but the most memorable souvenirs are free; a little scrap heap of granite chips sits beside the sugar house and you are entitled to take from the pile as much granite as you want under one condition: you must carry it away using only your hands. Granite weighs 166 pounds per cubic foot.

NORLANDS LIVING HISTORY CENTER

Your guide will introduce you to heifers Lili and Buttercup and other resident animals in the nineteenth century barn at Norlands Living History Center.

"**E**LIZA IS 3 YEARS OLD; HOW OLD WILL SHE BE IN 6 YEARS, IF SHE lives?"

> *Mental Arithmetic, a textbook, copyright 1874*

You first realize that there is something different about Norlands Living History Center as you drive onto the property and spot the sign that reads, "Horseless carriages—please park beside the church."

Located in rural western inland Maine, Norlands is a working 19th century farm which is unusual in that it may be experienced in a number of different ways.

If you would simply like to stroll the grounds of the circa 1870 farm and inspect a bygone way of life, you should plan to visit in July or August.

In addition to tours of the Victorian farmhouse, library, and barn, period "lessons" are offered in the one-room schoolhouse while oxen work the fields as they would have 120 years ago.

If you really wish to experience 19th century farm life, Norlands offers three day programs. Depending on your gender and the season, you may spend your waking hours churning butter in the kitchen, haying in the fields, baking pies, cutting ice, grinding corn meal, or feeding oxen.

To make the experience more realistic, 20th-century visitors assume the identities of 19th-century residents. You might become members of the Washburn family who actually lived at Norlands; or perhaps one of the neighboring Bradford or Waters families. But don't even think for a moment that when workaday tasks are done, you retire to a warm bed and a color television set at a nearby Marriott.

First off, there is no such thing as a nearby Marriott. The nearest sizable communities are Augusta, Auburn and Lewiston, each nearly 30 miles away along back roads. Second, a cushy room would defeat the purpose of the live-in experience. You will spend the three nights comfortably tucked on an authentic 1870 corn husk mattress and you'll be awakened at 6:30 A.M. by someone at the door with a pan of water. The water is for your morning sponge bath; forget about a hot shower. There is no running water at Norlands; the backyard outhouse is in great demand.

The three days in 1870s Maine are not all hardship and backbreaking labor. Time travelers are fed nine full meals and three evening snacks which consist of wholesome farm fresh foods like baked beans and ham, roast pork, home-made breads, plenty of vegetables, and a variety of pies—rhubarb in spring, and apple or pumpkin in fall. There is also a Saturday night quilting party or, sometimes, a husking bee, followed by a dance to the live sounds of Livermore's best traditional musicians. Line dances, square dances, and Virginia Reels are accompanied by fiddle and accordion. Expect Uncle Fred to show up with his harmonica.

This is the ultimate in living history. According to Terry Sharrer, the Curator for Agriculture at the Smithsonian Institution, this is the only program of its kind that is open to the general public in this country.

Norlands Living History Center is the brainchild of Billie Gammon, a Livermore grandmother, former school teacher, and history aficionado who boarded with former caretakers of Norlands when she was nineteen years old. Their tales about the Washburn family and Norlands resulted in her study of family papers and town records. When the Washburn family donated their farm for use as an educational center in 1974, Gammon was named director, a position she still holds.

Gammon must be credited for making Norlands a success. Schools send children of all ages here for "little time machine journeys." Older students, at the high school and university levels, are offered programs that are both academic and theatrical in nature.

At Norlands only two concessions are made to our modern era: toilet paper and window-screens. To prepare for an active adult live-in program, Gammon says participants "must be prepared to suffer a little," but adds that she's not out to surprise anyone. "Never, never would I have someone come without their knowing what they are in for."

Of course, people who don't wish to play such active roles can explore Norlands in a more relaxed fashion. As a day-visitor, you may view over two dozen family portraits that hang on the walls of the family memorial library, a Gothic-style stone structure replete with naves and so much stained glass that it is frequently mistaken for a church. Patriarch Israel Washburn and his wife Martha, the first residents of the farmstead, were very poor; Israel failed as the owner of a general store, and their seven sons and three daughters grew up in poverty.

The second generation Norland Washburns overcame impoverishment and achieved success as adults. Two were governors, four served in the United States House of Representatives, one was a U.S. senator, and another became Secretary of State under Ulysses S. Grant. In addition, two were distinguished businessmen—one of whom founded Gold Medal Flour. This generation also produced a writer and a Civil War hero. Charles, the fifth son, christened the family farm "Norlands," having derived the name from Tennyson's *Ballad of Orianna*.

Other rooms at Norlands contain many fine objects of interest, for instance the desk of Israel Washburn, Jr., governor of Maine in 1861, which dominates the front parlor and looks much like the one President Lincoln was using at the same time in the White House. The ladies' parlor contains many Victorian furnishings, among them a cameo sofa and ornamented candle holders.

In the kitchen, amid drying bundles of home-grown herbs and spices, is an array of antique kitchen utensils. Try to guess their uses.

As you leave the house, the portrait of Margaret Muzzy in the hallway will appear to follow you with it's eyes. If you then step into the barn, Sandy the ox, Darlene the pig, and the heifers Lili and Buttercup will also keep their eyes on you.

As mentioned earlier, a taste of 19th-century scholarship is offered in the little white schoolhouse. Guide Amy Coleman played schoolmarm for us when we visited. Twentieth-century youngsters were handed slates and chalk to doodle with while the rest of us were handed textbooks that were used 100 years ago by Maine's youth. In *Mental Arithmetic*, we read several problems including the one listed at the head of this section, sadly reminiscent of a time when many children didn't survive childhood.

A less morbid sample question was this: "A man sold a pig for 3 dollars and a sheep for 3 dollars; how many dollars did he receive for both?"

There is a third type of Norlands experience, which is a sort of happy medium between sightseeing and participation in the life of the farm. Four seasonal special events are offered annually. During Maple Days in March, a horse-drawn sled takes you into a nearby sugarbush. Pancake breakfasts and maple sundaes are on the menu.

Heritage Days, a four-day celebration taking place around the first day of summer is Norlands's biggest blowout. Crafts, from corn husk dolls to blacksmith's tools and blown glass, are demonstrated and sold. Food and music are in abundance and you can take an ox-drawn wagon ride or watch a parade of antique carriages.

The Autumn Celebration enables would-be farm hands to help make cider, thresh beans, and stuff mattresses with oats and straw. ("A few grasshoppers will get in there, too," laughs Gammon.) A noon meal of beans and brown bread, or beef and vegetable pie, is served to those with reservations.

Finally, Christmas at Norlands. You can sip from a wassail bowl, sing carols and observe craftspeople at work; you also tour the Washburn home, adorned for a 19th-century Christmas with a massive tree that has been trimmed with popcorn, cranberries, and other period decorations.

In addition, Norlands offers other seasonal activities. For example, sleigh rides and hay rides take visitors into the Maine countryside. After the ride you may enjoy hot chocolate while watching wool being spun into yarn, or join in old-fashioned games like "My Old Granny Doesn't Like Tea" or "Shouting Proverbs." How are they played? Visit Norlands and find out.

Location: From the Maine Turnpike (Interstate 495), exit 12 in Auburn, take Route 4 north to Route 108 east and follow the signs. **Admission** is charged. **Hours:** General tours of Norlands are offered daily in July and August. Three-day-long adult live-ins take place about seven times a year. **Allow** two hours for the general tour. **Information:** Norlands Living History Center, R.D. 2, Box 3395, Livermore Falls, ME 04254; (207) 897-2236 or 897-4366. **Note:** Billie Gammon also offers an additional live-in program where participants step back a century further to Maine in the late 1700s.

ADDITIONAL LISTINGS

NEW ENGLAND HAS MANY OTHER SITES MEMORIALIZING, HONORING and explaining the way we worked. Here's a list, excluding the places described in this book.

Mystic, CT. Mystic Seaport Museum. Year-round. (203) 572-0711.

Greenville, ME. Moosehead Marine Museum. June through September. (207) 695-2716.

Patten, ME. Lumberman's Museum. Memorial Day through Columbus Day. (207) 528-2650 or 528-2547.

Poland Spring, ME. Shaker Museum. Late May through Columbus Day. (207) 926-4597.

Searsport, ME. Penobscot Marine Museum. Memorial Day through mid-October. (207) 548-2529.

Fall River, MA. Battleship Massachusetts. Year-round. (508) 678-1100. Battleship Cove, (508) 678-1100; Marine Museum, (508) 674-3533.

Nantucket, MA. Nantucket Whaling Museum. May through mid-October. (508) 228-1894.

New Bedford, MA. New Bedford Whaling Museum. Year-round. (508) 997-0046.

North Andover, MA. Merrimack Valley Textile Museum. Year-round. (508) 686-0191.

Pittsfield, MA. Hancock Shaker Village. April through November. (413) 443-0188.

Milton, N.H. New Hampshire Farm Museum. Mid-June through mid-October. (603) 652-7840.

Newport, VT. American Maple Products Corporation. Year-round. (802) 334-6516.

Proctor, VT. Vermont Marble Exhibit. Year-round. (802) 459-3311.

St. Johnsbury, VT. Maple Grove Museum. May through October. (802) 748-5141.

Windsor, VT. American Precision Museum. Memorial Day through October. (802) 674-5781.

CASTLES
AND
MANSIONS

THEY HAD TO BE RICH AND MOST WERE ECCENTRIC, REASONS ENOUGH for them to build or buy what today might be called megahomes—multi-roomed mansions and Corinthian castles along New England's shores or high atop her hills.

As you tour the splendid interiors of these retreats of the wealthy, you observe the exotic as soon as you step in the door, whether the particular dwelling was built in the style of an English moat-fringed stronghold or an American-Victorian villa. Those who had money—especially new money—flaunted it. The evidence of those large bank accounts, trust funds, stock portfolios, and maybe even hard-earned incomes is over-whelming as you wander through the mirrored ballrooms and stately libraries. Stained glass windows, grand pianos, marble carved in a mul-titude of mythological formations, crystal chandeliers, silver place set-tings and exquisite china are the norm—what Tupperware and toaster ovens are to the rest of us.

But the tours of these homes are not limited to glimpses of luxury; they also unveil the people who danced in the ballrooms and dined from the china. Together, the stories of these privileged homeowners and their material riches reveal the life-styles of New England's own rich and famous.

Who might they be? There is the career military officer who bought the isolated castle nobody else wanted; the Maine man who made his millions in the streets of New Orleans and who came back home to enjoy them; the socialite who replaced a window in her mansion when she discovered that a neighbor was going to build a larger ballroom than her own. There is the Connecticut actor better known to most by his famous sleuthing alter ego, and the Boston shoe magnate who earned a fortune and lost every penny of it, dying as a destitute old man.

So enjoy these cathedrals of opulence, and for a few hours in your life, put yourself in a rich man's place.

GILLETTE CASTLE

Most people wouldn't think twice if they saw this castle perched upon a bluff overlooking the Rhine River. But visitors to New England do a double take when they see it sitting high above the Connecticut River.

THE NAME OF SHERLOCK HOLMES IS MORE FAMOUS THAN THAT OF William Gillette. But Gillette is due credit for immortalizing the name of the fictional detective with the Inverness cape and the deerstalker hat.

Gillette, son of a Connecticut senator, was an actor and a playwright who was most famous for his portrayal of the sleuth created by Arthur Conan Doyle. But while he played the role on stage for over three decades, much of his acclaim stemmed from the plays he wrote; he is credited with 13 original plays, seven adaptations and two collaborations. At the turn of the century, a dozen or so companies across the world were presenting Gillette's plays.

When the Hartford native was in his late 50s and looking for a home in which to settle for his last years, he took a spin up the Connecticut River on his houseboat, which he called *Aunt Polly*. Gillette had been planning to build a home near Greenport, Long Island, but the view of the tree-fringed ridge near the Chester-Hadlyme ferry slip about 30 miles down river from Hartford impressed him so much that he changed his plans.

The range of hills in that part of the lower Connecticut River Valley is known as the Seven Sisters, and Gillette decided to construct his dream home atop the southernmost hill, the Seventh Sister. Throughout his life, Gillette never referred to his home as a castle; it was always "Seventh Sister."

Local residents began to call it Gillette's castle. After all, it looks distinctly like a castle and it was patterned after a medieval Rhenish fortress, complete with battlements. Construction was started in 1914; five years and one million dollars later, the 66-year-old Gillette moved into his new Hadlyme home.

And what a home! Many are awestruck when they set foot inside the palatial 24-room structure. The atmosphere seems fitting for a spacious and toasty-warm hunting lodge. We visited once in mid-November, and a fire blazing in the living room fireplace reinforced that comfortable feeling.

Yet there is majesty as well as warmth in Seventh Sister. The living room is huge—50 feet long, 30 feet wide, with a ceiling 17.5 feet high. The walls are made of native stone and southern white oak, with raffia matting from the island of Java set into the wall paneling.

Many of the 47 doors and other interior furnishings are also made of carved oak. As you walk through the castle on your self-guided tour, keep your eyes on the wooden locks and bolts. None is like any other and all were devised by Gillette.

The locks were not the limit of Gillette's ingenuity. A system of releasing water in case of fire is activated at the pull of a carved oak appendage hanging over the balcony that looks onto the living room.

Gillette fashioned a bar in the cocktail lounge that can be opened and unlocked by inserting a metal strip through a back panel that appeared to be no more than a normal part of the décor. From his bedroom (which many visitors find surprisingly small), Gillette positioned two mirrors which permitted him to look downstairs into the living room. If he did not care for the guests who had arrived, or if he wasn't in the right frame of mind to speak to a certain party resting comfortably in the living room, he would simply remain upstairs. On other occasions, the actor would eye the situation downstairs and, as if on cue, enter at just the right moment.

Seventh Sister seldom bulged with visitors. Gillette rarely had guests for lunch or dinner, owing to the small size of the dining room, and usually limited his company to intimate friends from childhood, the theatre, and literary circles.

Friends, yes. But he didn't have a lifelong companion. He was married once, but his wife, Helen, died of a ruptured appendix at 28; honoring her wish, Gillette never remarried. Most of the time, there were more cats than people in the castle.

Like Ernest Hemingway, Mark Twain, and other American literary craftsmen, Gillette was fascinated with cats. He owned about 20 and gave them free reign of Seventh Sister. In the labyrinth of rooms, you come across evidence of his affection for felines: porcelain cats in the form of salt and pepper shakers, a pair of black cat bookends, and an illustration of a chorus of cats singing while another whiskered tabby accompanies them on the fiddle.

Photographs of Gillette's real-life cats decorate the walls. You see one cat resting on a wicker table. Another sits atop a step ladder while a third curls up on some good books. One wears a bib while sitting in an upright position at a dinner table; this photo is charmingly captioned, "Lunch is served." Then there is the bell used by Mrs. Babcock, Gillette's cook for 13 years, to call the cats together and tell them that dinner was served.

Other photos—of, for example, Gillette's houseboat and the private locomotives he owned and ran throughout his 122-acre property—join newspaper clippings and theatrical programs on the walls of many upstairs rooms. One room is an art gallery, and another has been rearranged to resemble Sherlock Holmes's fictional home at 221B Baker Street.

The library was Gillette's favorite room, but the conservatory off the living room downstairs may be most visitors' favorite. A miniature waterfall is the centerpiece in this abundant verdancy, and the fifty-year-old jade plant is one of the most unusual varieties. Like the library and the other favorite rooms of the actor and playwright, the conservatory is situated so it overlooks the Connecticut River. In fact, the view of the river might be reason enough for sightseers to drive up to the castle; it is stunning, especially on clear summer and brisk fall days.

Location: From Route 9, take exit 6 onto Route 148 east towards the car ferry. Take the ferry across the river and follow Geer Hill Road to the castle. Or from Route 9, take exit 7 onto Route 82; cross the bridge and take Route 82 to River Road west to the castle. **Admission** is charged. **Hours:** Daily, Memorial Day through Columbus Day; weekends, Columbus Day through weekend before Christmas. **Allow** one to two hours. **Information:** Gillette Castle State Park, 67 River Road, East Haddam, CT 06423; (203) 526-2336. **Note:** There are beautiful walking paths on the grounds and plenty of places for a leisurely picnic. Unfortunately, the castle tour is self-guided in summer. State park guides are stationed in various rooms to answer questions. Much of what you get out of your visit will depend greatly on what you ask the guides. A brochure for sale in the gift shop for a nominal charge can be purchased for background on the castle if you would like to know more.

HAMMOND CASTLE

Photo by Brian J. Vita

*Not your typical living room, this Gothic-style hall was the place where John
Hays Hammond read the newspaper while resting after a hard day's work.*

W
HAT KIND OF MAN WAS JOHN HAYS HAMMOND?

He had no children, but he let his nine cats use his 17th-century Spanish
leather-backed chairs as scratching posts.

He thought nothing of diving head first from his bedroom window into
his courtyard swimming pool.

He was often found reading a daily newspaper or an Edgar Allan Poe
novel while sitting comfortably in a reproduced 11th-century Byzantine
bishop's throne and listening to organ music.

He was a man who, fascinated with castles since his boyhood and as a
present to himself, built his own castle in 1926–29 on a point overlooking
the rocky Cape Ann coastline.

Hammond Castle in Gloucester, Massachusetts is a showcase for the
things you would find originals of in medieval Europe. There is a suit of
armor, a 14th-century Italian wrought iron bed, 15th-century fireplaces,
and what is claimed to be the largest pipe organ in any private residence
in the world. Hammond had no connection with the famous organ company

of the same name, however. The fact that the enormous pipe organ sits inside Hammond Castle is purely coincidental.

Hammond was the son of a mining engineer and made his fortune as an inventor. He held over 800 patents, second in number only to Thomas A. Edison, who accumulated 1,200 in his lifetime. Most of Hammond's inventions were sold to the military services and were components of bigger objects: an electric automobile starter, devices used in communicating ships' messages from one to another, and amplifers used in telephones, for example.

He also built the huge pipe organ in the great hall of the castle. But the pipes you notice first are ornamental, appearing high atop the walls as they would in an authentic castle; the organ actually has over 8,200 pipes, which can be seen in the end of the nave in the great hall, a room built to resemble the interior of a 13th-century Gothic cathedral. Except for the fake pipes, the room seems unnaturally bare. There are no tapestries or other wall hangings because Hammond wanted this room to be acoustically perfect, which meant nothing to absorb sounds.

The castle reveals a man who had a slightly off-center sense of humor. Hanging on the dining room wall is a tempera on wood painting called "The Martyrdom of Saint Romanus," depicting the torture and burial of a third-century Christian. Hammond usually sat at the table with his back towards the graphic display which, of course, meant that his dinner guests faced the victim having his tongue gouged out. After hearing the story behind the painting, guests were often served a special treat of beef tongue in brandied cherry sauce. Look at the seats of the chairs surrounding the table: claw marks and scratches prove that William Gillette wasn't the only cat-lover who lived in a castle.

The courtyard shows another example of the Hammond humor. It is modeled after a 15th-century French village built around Roman ruins. Look up from the courtyard and see pipes from which Hammond could create his own weather. From a light misting rain to a torrential downpour, he caused a variety of precipitation to fall from the artificial indoor heavens onto unsuspecting guests; mercifully, Hammond concocted these impromptu storms usually after they had been swimming in the courtyard pool.

In Rome, this pool would have been known as an impluvium, only a foot deep. Here, it is filled with ten feet of water. Fronting it is an actual second-century Roman marble sarcophagus made to bury a child. An unfinished carving on the top, however, indicates that it was never used; the white stones built into the walls in this room are ancient Roman tombstones.

Following your tour, you can climb part way to the top of the castle tower, where photographs of Hammond, his yacht, and his pets are displayed. If you have never seen a $2,000 dog, pay attention to the picture of Boris, one of the Hammond canines who was kidnapped and held for $2,000 ransom. You will also learn that Hammond Castle had its own official name: *Abbadia Mare*, which translated from Latin means, "abbey by the sea."

Location: From Route 128, take exit 14 onto Route 133 (Essex Avenue) towards Gloucester. At Gloucestor Harbor, turn right onto Route 127 (Western Avenue), then bear left onto Hesperus Avenue; the castle is at 80 Hesperus Avenue. **Admission** is charged. **Hours:** April through November, daily; weekends only the rest of the year. **Allow** 45 minutes for the tour. **Information:** Hammond Castle, 80 Hesperus Avenue, Gloucester, MA 01930; (508) 283-2080. **Note:** Organ concerts and other special events are scheduled regularly.

THE ASTORS' BEECHWOOD

Courtesy: Beechwood

Your admission tickets are tagged "calling cards" at Beechwood. Leave them at the door and enter the world of turn-of-the-century Newport society. Here, kitchen workers have some fun taste testing a dessert to be served at one of Mrs. Astor's dinners.

THE LATE ROD SERLING OF "THE TWILIGHT ZONE" FAME MIGHT HAVE introduced you to the Astors' Beechwood mansion in Newport, Rhode Island, like this:

"Consider if you will. Two tourists in the midst of a day or a weekend or a week-long visit to the splendiferous mansions on Newport's renowned Bellevue Avenue.

"Their excursion has been rather ordinary so far. They have examined the summer palaces of America's commercial royalty, one after another, to the point of becoming jaded. One mansion slowly fades into the next, one crystal chandelier blends into another.

"But as they enter the house at 580 Bellevue, things suddenly seem a bit peculiar. Grover Cleveland is president of the United States. George Bush hasn't been born. Electricity is the newest gimmick. The Canon AE-1 camera hanging around one of the tourist's neck is a curiosity, a mysterious looking 'picture box.' And the two tourists feel naked standing in public with their legs exposed in cut-off jeans.

"The mansion they have entered is properly called The Astors' Beechwood. But to our two friends, they might have stepped back in time to a place we might just as well label . . . The Twilight Zone."

Maybe you don't unlock the door to Beechwood with the key to imagination. But compared to Newport's other famous mansions, this one is a real diversion. It brings visitors face to face with what Serling might have called "a shadowy tip of reality."

Beechwood is unlike the summer cottages where employees interpret the past. Here, they act out the roles of Mrs. Caroline Astor's housemaids, servants, cooks, and distinguished guests. They don't tell you about 1890s Newport; they live 1890s Newport!

A formally dressed young man introduces himself as a servant, takes our "calling cards" (a.k.a. our admission tickets) and greets us as if we were the upper crust members of Mrs. Astor's exclusive New York 400.

He ushers us into a reception room where we sit in front of a "new invention from Mr. Edison," a visual presentation of the Astor family background. We hear the true story of John Jacob Astor, who made his millions in the fur trade and at one time owned one-fifth of the island of Manhattan.

The Mrs. Astor we are visiting in Beechwood is the former Caroline Webster Schermerhorn, married to William Backhouse Astor, Jr., grandson of the founder of the fortune.

It was Mrs. Astor who devised the fashionable and famous New York 400. She and her secretary, Ward McAllister, compiled the names of 231 families and individuals that comprised these 400 pillars of society. Why 400? The capacity of the Beechwood ballroom, at one time largest in Newport, is (surprise) 400.

As the footman leads us out of the screening room and into the foyer, he tells us we can expect to see a home of "simple elegance."

"The Astors are not like the Vanderbilts, who are so ostentatious. Don't you agree?" he says with his own hint of snootiness.

But he has a point. This is one mansion that won't overwhelm you. It reflects a quiet Georgian, as opposed to an ornate Victorian, style.

The ballroom is a perfect expression of Beechwood's muted decor. When we enter the room, Captain Horatio Rumprear, a member of the British Royal Navy who is in Newport as part of an exchange program with the War College, replaces our first guide, and asks a visitor with an adolescent son how he made his fortune.

"Have you made some earnings from a silver mine?" Rumprear inquires.

The father wrinkles his eyebrows and looks bewildered.

Rumprear is more specific. He calls the visitor's attention to the braces on his son's teeth and admiringly asks, "Is this an indication of the fortune you have gotten from a silver mine?"

The boy blushes, the father laughs.

"Oh, I see," nods Rumprear. "You actually have spent a silver mine."

The father agrees, laughing.

Rumprear flirts harmlessly with a young woman on the tour and assumes she will be at the ball to be held later in the evening.

"And how many gowns did you bring with you?" he purrs to the pretty tourist.

"Four," she quietly responds, guessing at a satisfactory answer.

"Oh, so you are only staying for the evening," he comments.

Rumprear tells us about the ballroom, with its symmetrical and reflectional appearance, due in part to its more than 450 mirrors and the mirrored effect of the relief panels on the ceiling. We then pass through the dining room, where 10) to 20-course meals are served, before heading up the stairs to the second story.

Children climb the servants' staircase, separated from their parents, just as they would have in late Victorian society. Meanwhile, in the public portion of the house, adult male guests are asked to precede women up the stairs, making sure that they cannot catch a lecherous glimpse of the ladies' ankles.

On the second floor we find head housekeeper Fraulein Helga Von Schlepin, 32 years old and a native of Heidelberg, Germany, slumped over in Mrs. Astor's sitting room, obviously well-settled in the arms of Morpheus. She awakes startled, but is ready to continue where Captain Rumprear left off, with a fervent denial that she was actually sleeping.

She escorts us to the rooms where we—Mrs. Astor's guests—will supposedly be staying the night. We see where Mrs. Astor has had a window in the Peach Room removed and filled in so her guests will not be offended by a view of the sweaty workers laboring on the new Rosecliff mansion being built next door. (There is a nasty rumor that Mrs. Oelrichs, the owner of Rosecliff, is building a ballroom larger than Mrs. Astor's—the true reason for removing the window. Mrs. Astor, of course, explicitly denies it.)

Fraulein Von Schlepin lets the visiting ladies in on a little secret as she ushers us into another lady's guest room called the Violet Room, named for Rhode Island's state flower. By looking out the window, sharp-eyed female guests can keep an eye on the gentlemen callers arriving at the front door. Depending on how attractive they find the men, the guests can stay in their rooms or rush (trying all the while to look demure) downstairs to meet them at the door.

Peter Dedlock, the tenth serving man, takes over for the housekeeper and leads us up to the servants' rooms on the third floor. We peer out a window at the Chinese Tea House in the back of the Vanderbilts' Marble House. Dedlock talks disdainfully of the suffragettes who meet in the tea house, where they smoke cigarettes and talk about the ludicrous idea of voting. The 18-year-old footman then turns to a male visitor, dressed in casual shorts and says, "And I see you have taken to wearing bloomers, too."

"Now," continues Dedlock, "I know you ladies have never been inside a kitchen, so if you get the vapors, tell me and I will be sure to bring you some smelling salts."

None of the guests is afflicted with the vapors, but as we enter the kitchen downstairs, we are soothed anyway with cups of strawberry tea, brewed just for us in the Astor kitchen.

After a look inside the kitchen with its gas stove and other gas appliances ("I don't think this electricity will catch on," Dedlock sighs; "when you turn it off, where does it go?") we are shown to the exit with assurances that we will be back at Beechwood for the grand ball that evening.

Once we set foot outdoors in the brisk Newport air, George Bush really is president and our 35-millimeter cameras seem common. Our automobiles are unspectacular, and we are more interested in getting a parking space in town than finding out what ingredients go into the Fillet de Saumon Mornay that Mrs. Astor will be serving this coming evening.

But it does seem as if we had departed from the late 20th century for an hour, transported back to a time of parasols and band concerts and ladies waving Oriental fans—as if we had actually been in . . . The Twilight Zone.

Location: The Astors' Beechwood is at 580 Bellevue Avenue in Newport. **Admission** is charged. **Hours:** June through December, daily. **Allow** up to an hour. **Information:** The Astors' Beechwood, 580 Bellevue Avenue, Newport, RI 02840; (401) 846-3772. **Note:** Unlike many other sites open to the general public, Beechwood will close its doors when a private party or wedding is scheduled. We recommend calling in advance before planning a special trip here.

VICTORIA MANSION

Courtesy: Victoria Mansion

The epitome of Victoriana is this Portland, Maine mansion—home of a Maine man who made his fortune in Louisiana.

P ORTLAND'S VICTORIA MANSION IS A RARITY AMONG NOTEWORTHY NEW England palaces open to the public. It is named neither for its builder or one of its long-time owners, nor for a benefactor who saved it from razing.

The Victoria in the name of this Danforth Street domain refers to the queen and the architectural period labeled for her. When this landmark was about to face the wrecking ball to make room for a gas station, two Augusta, Maine natives—Dr. William Holmes and his sister, Clara Holmes—purchased it. They admired both the queen and the style; the Victoria Society of Maine was formed, and the Victoria Mansion was named.

Like many famous subjects, this one uses a stage name. It is also known as the Morse-Libby House, an awkward but more accurate label. A Maine native who made his fortune as a hotelier in New Orleans, Ruggles Sylvester Morse, built this house. And it was the family of Joseph Ralph Libby who followed the Morses as the last residents.

Morse and his wife, Olive Ring Merrill Morse, had this Italian villa-style structure built as a summer home away from the oppressive heat and humidity of Louisiana. Ultimately, it would become their full-time residence. As a man of modest means, Morse was justifiably proud of his success and desired a home to be a monument to his new-found status. He hired distinguished architect Henry Austin (the Yale University Library in New Haven, Connecticut is one of his monumental works) to design his home, had seven Carrara marble fireplaces custom shipped to Portland, and brought several artisans to Portland to carve other moldings for the house; the artisans lived in Portland from the time the building was begun in 1858 until the last bronze chandelier was in place around 1860.

Thanks to the generosity of the Morses' heirs, who returned many of the original family possessions, you see Victoria Mansion today in its full 19th-century eclectic glory. The Victorian interior is as luxurious as any home north of Newport; the multi-colored frescoes, the carved woodwork, and the dazzling stained glass are the most memorable features.

Many sightseers are awestruck by the 19th-century technique known as *trompe l'oeil* ("to deceive the eye"), optical illusions that are seen throughout the home, along with other Victorian touchstones, such as cabbage roses, cherubs and other nude figures.

Our guide said as she pointed to her neck, "The Victorians had many naked statues even though they buttoned up to here. It was okay to be naked as long as it was art."

The first room visitors see in this dazzling home is the reception room. The cherubs and dancing maidens carved intricately into the marble fireplace proclaim the period of the room, while allegorical figures on the ceilings represent the arts—music, literature, painting, and architecture—and identify the owner as a man of culture. Here is a prime example of *trompe l'oeil:* the ceiling paintings seem three-dimensional, and what you may think is wood on the walls is really painted plaster.

The reception room and the drawing room depart from the expected

Victorian mode in one sense: both feel light and airy, especially the pre-dominantly gold and white drawing room.

But the library brings you back into the realm of somber Victoriana. Morse thought this room should look dignified, and did away with any traces of frivolity. The dining room, paneled in American oak, also appeared dark and somber until the late 1980s when a restoration project removed 120 years of dirt and grime. Exposed now is painted plaster. Looking much like light-colored wood, it is especially beautiful when the massive chandelier is lit. In keeping with the room's use, designer Gustav Herter, a German immigrant designer from New York, had fish, game, and to honor Morse's home state, lobster carved into the woodwork.

The Gothic-style library returns the visitor to the realm of dark, heavy Victoriana. Sharp angles rule in the imposing dark chestnut room. Maine outdoors scenes, tableaus of fishing, hunting, and sailing ornament the engraved globes of the bronze chandelier. Most of the books in the black, walnut bookcases are part of the collection of the Victoria Society, governing body of the mansion. There are some original volumes, however, including Gibbon's *History of Rome* and Bancroft's *History of the United States*.

The second floor has the guest rooms, a smoking room and a sitting room. No women were permitted in the smoking room, also known as the Turkish Room because of the heavy Ottoman influence. Morse put his mark on the design of his house in various ways, one of which is a room identified primarily with the man of the house on each floor. The first floor has the library; the second, the smoking room; and the third, a billiards room.

The antithesis of the smoking room is the second floor family sitting room. It is less formal than the stiff downstairs rooms and it was the playroom for visiting children as well as the place for the annual Christmas tree.

A rare, two-story bronze chandelier, an enormous mahogany and copper bath tub (marvelled our guide, "You can put all of Coxey's Army in it."), and a double-basin sink with porcelain bowls decorated with hand-painted flowers in the guest bedroom are other second-floor highlights.

Location: Victoria Mansion is at 109 Danforth Street, between State and High Streets in Portland, Maine. From Interstate 95 heading north, take exit 6A south onto Forest Street. At the first intersection, take a right; this road will become State Street. The road is long and climbs and curves. After you pass Mercy Hospital on the right, turn left onto Danforth Street. **Admission** is charged. **Hours:** June through September, Tuesday through Saturday; and Sunday afternoon. Closed major holidays.

Allow 45 minutes. **Information:** Victoria Mansion, 109 Danforth Street, Portland, ME 04101; (207) 772-4841. **Note:** The restoration might still be in progress when you visit. Don't let this deter you, especially since it may afford some insight into the hard work of restoring a historic home.

CASTLE IN THE CLOUDS

Thomas Plant's extravagant Castle In the Clouds sits high above Lake Winnipesaukee, a luxurious millionaire's mansion built among nature's best creations.

Photo by Michael Schuman

Thomas Gustave Plant. The name is a metaphor for the fortunes and foibles of free enterprise: just as quickly as Plant's resourcefulness earned him 21 million dollars, his poor business sense left him a pauper.

His legacy lives in a lush stone home with a Spanish slate roof overlooking Lake Winnipesaukee in Moultonborough, New Hampshire. Plant called this summer retreat Lucknow, but it is better known to New Hampshire tourists as the Castle in the Clouds.

A Bath, Maine native who carved a career in Boston, Plant retired early and lived to regret it. He was born into a poor Bath family in 1859 and quit school 13 years later to support himself. Since the local ship building industry provided little interest to Plant, he took a job in a Boston shoe factory. Plant's ideas and inventions were later incorporated into the factory's systems and, finally, Plant purchased the factory. As the years progressed, Plant expanded his business and owned several more shoe manufacturing facilities.

Thomas Plant's ideas for the workplace show a man who was far ahead of his time. He furnished his factories with such extracurricular assets as gymnasiums, picnic areas, and libraries. One factory in Jamaica Plain outside Boston boasted a swimming pool. He started a vocational training program that paid young people while they learned a trade, and he replaced stairways with ramps so items could be delivered by employees on roller skates.

While still in his fifties, Plant decided to retire, and searched the world for a perfect place to spend the rest of his years. With the help of a relative he chose a spot high in the Ossipee Mountains; it afforded the type of view people would pay money to see.

And they do. Today, summer and fall visitors to the Granite State pay admission as they enter the property at the base of the hill. So even if you don't wish to tour the castle, you pay the same amount as those who are yearning to.

On the guided tour, you see this millionaire's playthings as you hear the unfortunate chronicle of his life. He and his second wife, Olive Dewey Plant, 26 years his junior, moved into Lucknow in 1914. (He divorced his first wife in 1912.) Expenses were not spared in the creation of this man's castle. A price tag of over $7 million was placed on its construction.

Inside are testaments to Plant's innovative concepts and eccentric tastes. Carved griffins—mythological creatures that are part lion and part eagle—guard the entrance to the library, one of Plant's favorite rooms. A statuette, a bust, and a portrait of Napoleon decorate the library; Plant stood 5'1" and admired the French emperor. Before leaving the library, notice the gold marble fireplace. The chimney sits to one side, allowing residents and guests a superb view of New Hampshire's outdoors through a window just above a blazing fire.

Symmetrically-veined Italian marble squares flank the fireplace in the game room. (Wait until you hear about Plant's troubles in finding them!) In this large chamber is a monstrous keyboard instrument designed by the Aeolian Organ Company, standing 21 feet deep by 12 feet wide by 13 feet high, which can be operated by skilled hands and by the magic of player rolls.

Octagons were another Plant passion. The dining room, the master bedroom, and both guest rooms all have eight sides. The master bedroom has fewer frills than the other bedrooms, but its simplicity is compensated for by the needle shower in the bathroom. Horizontal and vertical pipes, pierced with holes in selected spots, spray jets of water from all directions.

The castle's hand-painted windows are dazzling, and the seven skylights utilizing the sun's warmth prove that Plant's ideas would be practical too far in the future for his contemporaries to enjoy. "People are paying megabucks for those today," said a man on our tour as he eyed the skylights and shook his head disgustedly.

What happened to this man who built factories and a spectacular home in the hills? How did he lose a fortune?

His first years at Lucknow gave no hints of impending doom. Plant donated plenty to charity in 1917, including a home for the elderly in Bath, Maine in memory of his mother. He also expanded his interests, building a country club on nearby property in 1921. (The membership fee was $2,500. No liquor was sold, no swearing was permitted, and no person weighing over 200 pounds could belong.)

You hear the rest of Plant's saga on the tour. By the 1930s, his castle was heavily mortgaged. He entered the hospital in 1941, virtually penniless. He died on July 25 of that year at the age of 82 and was buried in a simple grave in Bath. Loyal friends paid his burial expenses.

What caused this journey from bottom to top to bottom? Poor investments, including costly real estate dealings combined with a high standard of living, plus the crash, chipped away at Plant's castle of contentment. Perhaps the worst mistake Plant made was investing heavily in Russian bonds . . . just prior to the Russian revolution in 1917.

Location: Castle in the Clouds at Castle Springs is located off Route 171 about six miles south of Moultonborough along the eastern shore of Lake Winnipesaukee. **Admission** is charged. **Hours:** Mid-May through mid-October. **Allow** 45 minutes. **Information:** Castle in the Clouds, P.O. Box 131, Moultonborough, NH 03254; (603) 476-8844. **Note:** Horseback riding is available on the grounds. Tours of the water bottling plant are offered.

WILSON CASTLE

It is said that Herbert Wilson bought his Vermont castle for "one dollar plus other considerations." It is believed that he got his money's worth.

COLONEL HERBERT L. WILSON WAS IN THE RIGHT PLACE AT THE RIGHT time. Either that or he was just a little crazy. After all, during the waning years of the Great Depression, people weren't waiting in line to buy a 32-room castle high up in the Vermont hills. But Wilson, a career Army man and electrical engineer, didn't care about the others. He truly believed his home should be his castle.

Nobody—nobody who is telling anyway—knows how much the colonel paid for the most famous home in Proctor, Vermont. The guide says he paid "one dollar plus other considerations." One assumes he got his money's worth.

It is known that the cost to build the castle in 1867 was $1.3 million, and it was the creation of a Dr. Johnson, a Vermonter who wanted his British-born wife to feel at home.

Accordingly, he attempted in every possible way to make the house look authentic. The facade is set with English brick and marble. There are turrets and parapets, and 84 stained glass windows. But while the home must have pleased her, it didn't fulfill its purpose. After a few years, the two of them left the house; it is believed they moved back to England.

A succession of owners followed until the Wilsons took possession. The property remains in their family, and their daughter still lives there year-round; it is not unusual to find her chatting with guests who come to tour the house.

This home is filled with treasures worthy of a fine arts museum, among them: a Chinese scroll dating from the year 927; a Louis XVI crown jewel case of deep dark blue; a teakwood statue of a Burmese dancer that dates back to ca. 1570 (the dancer's long hair is tied with a knot in back meaning she is unmarried); a Louis XV papal chair; and a massive stained glass window weighing about one ton that is situated halfway up the main staircase.

Our tour guide, a young law student named Judy, who "grew up just down the street," made certain that we noticed how most of the castle's stained glass windows relate to the purpose of the rooms in which they are situated. Some are allegorical; others pay tribute to individuals or ideas. The three in the library portray Aladdin's Lamp of Learning, William Shakespeare, and the beehive of industriousness.

Representations of fish, fruit and pudding are in the dining room stained glass, while in the French Renaissance-style drawing room, the mood is set by windows illustrating a woman playing a harpsichord and others looking dreamy, lost in wonder; they represent music and thought. The English window sandwiched between those latter two shows the Thames River in London, complete with swans, fog, and the famous buildings along its banks; it was obviously put there to remind the castle's first lady of home.

Other symbols denote their respective rooms: lyres grace both the frescoed ceiling and the French cut velvet chairs in the music room, for instance.

Many of the castle's features are simply ornamental, serving to make it appear realistic. In medieval England, turrets were built for defensive purposes; here, they seem to have been constructed to look genuine. Some have been turned into sitting rooms or bathrooms. The Wilson Castle staff, employing Yankee ingenuity, made one into a sitting area, where you can see anything from a mounted boar's head to an antique chair waiting to be reupholstered.

There is an anomaly in this castle-turned-house, however. Closets were built into some upstairs rooms, even though they are a distinct American feature, rarely found in European castles or palaces.

The walls of the art gallery are filled with paintings, all by regional artists and all for sale. When we toured, bucolic Vermont landscapes and still lifes were being shown, priced between $45 and $175. There may be other styles in other price ranges when you visit.

The scenery that inspires so many of the Green Mountain State's talented artists competes with the European and Far Eastern interior for your admiration. From the veranda you face a commanding panorama of the Killington Mountain Range, framed by the proscenium arches of the porch. As Judy led us onto the veranda, she pointed out the highly unusual swing with a flat, wooden bottom and chains on the sides that are hooked into the ceiling. She called it an English levelling swing, more than likely built by the original owners, and since there is room for two on board, probably used for courting. As the name implies, it swings level to the ground, so a proper Victorian young lady's petticoats wouldn't be exposed.

Judy offered us a chance to give the swing a whirl, but nobody in our group was brave enough to do so. We did, however, take advantage of the opportunity to put our fingers in the mouth of the ferocious carved wooden lion jutting from the dining room fireplace, appreciating the detail in the carving. She also let us stroke the Honduras mahogany ribs on the Grand Reception Hall fireplace which, as Judy said, "feels more like glass than wood." We were impressed that at this castle, one can touch as well as look, a liberty not common in the majority of historic museums.

Location: To reach Wilson Castle, take Route 4 west of Rutland. About a half mile past the junction with Route 3, take a right onto West Proctor Road and continue until you reach the castle. **Admission** is charged. **Hours:** Daily, May through October. **Allow** 45 minutes for the tour. **Information:** Wilson Castle, P.O. Box 290, Center Rutland, VT 05736; (802) 773-3284. **Note:** Picnic tables are on the grounds. While the Wilson Castle staff is generous with its "do touch" policy, this does not apply to children (or adults) with chocolate-covered hands. Touch only when permitted to do so, use your discretion, and watch your children.

OOD-MATHEWS MANSION

Courtesy: Lockwood-Mathews Mansion

This magnificent Connecticut mansion boasts 50 rooms and is dominated by an imposing 42-foot high rotunda.

THERE IS NO EVIDENCE THAT THE MUSIC ROOM OF LEGRAND LOCKWOOD'S gabled and turretted Norwalk, Connecticut mansion ever contained even one musical instrument. Of course, that didn't matter much, since the *nouveau riche* Lockwood had the room designed, more or less, just to show off.

If LeGrand Lockwood came back today, he'd doubtless be delighted to see that the music room is just one of several rooms that look as lavish today as they did when the final piece of ebony inlay was applied to the boxwood doors in 1868. He might not be as pleased to know that he shares top billing when it comes to the name of his custom-built palace. The Lockwood-Mathews Mansion hosted LeGrand Lockwood for only four years, from 1868 until his death from pneumonia in 1872; his wife lost the property to foreclosure two years later. On the other hand, the Mathews family made a home in this Victorianized French chateau-style mansion for three generations, from 1876 to 1938.

Like many Victorian era millionaires, LeGrand Lockwood was a self-made man. And like many, he watched it all slip away. His business, as Calvin Coolidge said 60 years later, "was business." Lockwood made his fortune as head of his own banking firm and as a heavy investor in railroad and steamship concerns. He successfully promoted U.S. war bonds abroad and was elected treasurer of the New York Stock Exchange.

Lockwood hadn't been in his magnificent mansion a year when on September 24, 1869, the price of gold plummeted. Thanks to the manipulation of the gold market by Jay Gould (sort of the Ivan Boesky of his day), Lockwood's banking firm was ruined. To cover his losses, Lockwood was forced to mortgage his estate and sell $10 million worth of railroad stock. For needed funds, his widow sold his paintings and other rare possessions following his death.

The next owner, Charles D. Mathews, was an importer from New York City. The Mathews family altered much of the mansion interior, but made no structural changes to the outside. Restoration work began in 1966 and continues on the upper floors to this day. Photos of the mansion taken in the Lockwoods' time serve as valuable guides for the restorers.

The hub of the fifty-room house is the rotunda. Forty-two feet high and circled by a second floor balcony, it is an imposing room that the visitor will long remember. The rotunda is thought to have been used by the Lockwoods as both a ballroom and as a repository for the owner's many paintings and sculptures; today it is used as a showplace for rotating art exhibits. When we visited, "From Ads to Art: Nineteenth-Century Prints," featuring everything from political ads to a *Folies Bergere* poster, was on view.

There is a natural reflex to look up towards the skylight while standing in the rotunda, but we would be remiss if we didn't urge the visitor to look down as well. The rotunda's parquet floor consists of five different kinds of wood interlocked in a pattern that denotes the traffic areas with accent lines. Such complex craftsmanship rules the mansion's design. The library's parquet floor also consists of five kinds of wood while the ceiling is made from black walnut panels with blue, rose and gold centers. The papier mâché wallpaper was created to play tricks with your eyes and looks like Moroccan leather. Please don't neglect to notice the library double doors, each garnished with etched glass.

The dining room, with its columns, pediments and chandeliers, might be the mansion's showiest. On the ceiling are frescoes depicting fruits of many colors while the carpeting shows off *fleur-de-lis* designs. The double door of iron and wood opens to reveal a vault for the protection of the residents' silver from fire and theft.

In other rooms, Victoriana rules. Venus plays with cherubs on the drawing room ceiling while frescoes of birds and flower-filled vases give the cozy card room a romantic feel. The original Waterford crystal chandelier affords the card room a touch of elegance.

Another common Victorian touch, though not as well known as cherubs and flowers, was Middle Eastern decor. In Maine, Portland's Victoria Mansion (Chapter 28) boasts an Ottoman smoking room while the Victorian-era home of the painter Frederick Church looks as if it had been plucked from ancient Persia and placed high on a Hudson River bluff in upstate New York. So too did the Lockwoods incorporate a bit of Middle Eastern flair into their mansion. The Moorish Room with its typical horseshoe design and diamond-shaped tiles over the fireplace is thought to have served as a second story drawing room for the use of guests.

After the Moorish Room, the visitor enters the music room. Though the Lockwood and Mathews families played no instruments, they did manage to confirm the room's name with classical depictions of harps, flutes, drums and other instruments on the paneled ceiling. However, the most notable curiosity in the music room is the fireplace; the flues are off to the sides of the fireplace and guide Tony Franks often mystifies children by asking where the smoke goes.

Today one can hear the sweet sounds of music in the mansion. Four second-floor rooms serve as showplaces for the Music Box Society, a nonprofit group that collects and displays these tuneful antiques. In this museum-within-a-museum, you can hear the dulcet sounds of classic European- and American-made music boxes from the 19th and early 20th centuries as well as English barrel organs and player piano rolls.

With the help of youngsters on our tour, guide Joe Chesaitis set the workings in motion on about a half-dozen music boxes, demonstrating the variety in sound and purpose. The contrast was striking between the delicate tones of the European cylinder music boxes and the honky tonk raucousness of the ca. 1890 player piano that at one time accompanied the screams of children in an English ice cream parlor. Finally there is the Edison Company cylinder phonograph, dated 1899, which Chesaitis lamented, "put us out of business."

Though much of the second floor is still being restored, the Italian marble sinks in the master bathroom and the fireplace mantel with its inlaid mosaic panel of birds are well worth the climb up the staircase. The carved lions' heads and inlaid wainscotting on the landing alone make it a masterpiece. The price tag for the staircase, according to Tony

Franks, is estimated at $50,000, pocket change when considering the $2 million cost of the entire mansion.

Lockwood didn't plan his mansion solely for show. In the basement is proof that even a Victorian-era millionaire could have the same passions as those of more modest means. Under the brick arches on the bottom floor were two bowling alleys. At some future date, the basement will be restored.

The Lockwoods enjoyed other sporting pursuits as well. There were two billiard rooms on the first floor to which no women were admitted. Women could often be found in the small card room while the men were chalking up their cues. No billiard tables are found there today; however, for it is in these rooms that a ten minute slide presentation on the mansion and its residents is shown.

Location: The Lockwood-Mathews Mansion is at 295 West Avenue in Norwalk. Going south on Interstate 95, take exit 15 and turn right at the end of the ramp. Turn right at the first driveway after the ramp onto the mansion grounds. Going north on Interstate 95, take exit 14. The ramp extends two blocks to West Avenue; there's a stoplight at this intersection. Turn left and proceed under the interstate, then turn right onto the first driveway onto the mansion grounds. **Admission** is charged. **Hours:** Year-round, Tuesday through Friday late morning and early afternoon, and Sunday afternoon. **Allow** an hour and a half for the tour. **Information:** Lockwood-Mathews Mansion Museum, 295 West Avenue, Norwalk, CT 06850; (223) 838-1434. **Note:** The museum runs a quality gift shop stocked with handicrafts, music boxes and books on Victorian America.

ADDITIONAL LISTINGS

Hᴏᴡ ᴅᴏᴇꜱ ᴏɴᴇ ᴅɪꜱᴛɪɴɢᴜɪꜱʜ ʙᴇᴛᴡᴇᴇɴ ᴀ ᴍᴀɴꜱɪᴏɴ ᴀɴᴅ ᴀ ʙɪɢ ʜᴏᴜꜱᴇ? Or decide what's a palace rather than a castle? Here are more mansions, excluding those described elsewhere in this book.

Gloucester, MA. Beauport. Mid-May to mid-October (508) 283-0800.

Holyoke, MA. Wistariahurst. Year round. (413) 534-2216.

Marblehead, MA. Jeremiah Lee Mansion and King Hooper Mansion. Lee mansion open mid-May through mid-October. Hooper mansion open year round. Lee mansion, (617) 631-1069; Hooper, (617) 631-2608.

Stockbridge, MA. Naumkeag. Memorial Day through Columbus Day. (413) 298-3239.

Portsmouth, NH. Wentworth-Coolidge Mansion. Memorial Day through Labor Day. (603) 436-6607.

Bristol, RI. Blithewold Gardens and Arboretum. Mid-April through October. (401) 253-2707. (Gardens open year round.)

Newport, RI. Mansions operated by the Preservation Society of Newport County: The Breakers, Kingscote, Marble House, Chateau-Sur-Mer, The Elms, Rosecliff. Days and hours differ depending on individual mansion. (401) 847-1000 (information for all above mansions).

Newport, RI. Belcourt Castle. Year round, limited schedule in winter. (401) 846-0669.

Providence, RI. John Brown House. March through December; by appointment in the winter. (401) 331-8575.

North Bennington, VT. Park-McCullough House. Mid-May through October. (802) 442-5441.

SPORTS AND LEISURE

Oﾠᴜʀ ʟᴇɪsᴜʀᴇ ᴛɪᴍᴇ ɪs ɪᴍᴘᴏʀᴛᴀɴᴛ. ᴛʜᴇʀᴇ ᴊᴜsᴛ ɴᴇᴠᴇʀ sᴇᴇᴍs ᴛᴏ ʙᴇ enough of it.

New Englanders can be thanked for giving the world some of its favorite pastimes.

We originated basketball, we made tennis a big-time sport in America, and our slopes have attracted many expert skiers. Although we can't claim baseball or football as our own, we have bred many athletes who have excelled on the diamond and gridiron.

When we haven't participated on the field or watched from the recliner, we have spent our spare time poring over the games or playing with the toys that have diverted an entire planet. We can be more than a little proud that some of the best have been produced right here. They are still made here, including those high-technology toys with keyboards and video screens.

The visitor needn't be a sports diehard to enjoy our Halls of Fame and sports museums.

Many worthwhile hours can be spent looking at New England's collections of athletic memorabilia, toys, games and dolls. Some bring back personal memories; others would be too old for your great-grandfather to remember. In these places, our biggest leisure-time industries are memorialized. And, as I found out, even computer haters—or former computer haters—will enthusiastically enjoy our new hi-tech toys.

Have fun!

NAISMITH MEMORIAL BASKETBALL HALL OF FAME

Hot dogs, apple pie and baseball are America's emblems. But a visit to the Hall of Fame can make you feel that basketball is really the nation's pastime. Here a youngster tests his skills at "Shoot-Out."

Photo by Michael Schuman

T HE TIME WAS THE "GAY '90S." WESTWARD EXPANSION HAD SLOWED. America was now settled from coast to coast. We had run out of frontier and needed to turn inward to expand.

It was an age of optimism. We were becoming a world power. We began to ride in automobiles. We danced the cakewalk. We even took our own photographs with George Eastman's picture box.

It was in this spirit that Dr. James Naismith, an ordained minister, YMCA instructor and native son of Ontario, Canada, developed a new sport at the School for Christian Workers in Springfield, Massachusetts.

It wasn't an easy task. Naismith's students, whom he labeled "incorrigibles," had become bored with such dull indoor winter activities as weight room and medicine ball workouts. He was failing miserably in his attempt to devise a pastime that would interest them. One idea after another flopped.

Sitting in his office, he sighed, "I was a thoroughly disheartened and discouraged young instructor. Below I could hear the boys in the locker room having a good time. They were giving expression to the very spirit I was trying to evoke."

Naismith made a final effort. His plan called for a soccer ball and two boxes. When the janitor at the school, today known as Springfield College, could not find the cartons for which Naismith asked, the instructor decided to use two peach baskets. They were attached to the galleries at each end of the gymnasium, 10 feet off the floor. Today, 10 feet is still the regulation height for the nets used in basketball.

When the Naismith Memorial Basketball Hall of Fame opened in 1968, it was only natural that it was located at the site where the game was invented. But the campus of Springfield College is well off Interstate 91, not readily accessible to tourists breezing up the highway toward the recreation and sightseeing areas of New Hampshire and Vermont. Through the years, another problem developed: a shortage of space for a constantly expanding museum.

With help from the Commonwealth of Massachusetts and the Springfield Central Business District, Inc., the Hall of Fame was relocated in the summer of 1985 to a new location, near downtown with easy access to Interstate 91. The new home is as different from the old brick structure on Alden Street as Larry Bird is from a bench warmer on the Utah Jazz.

With the new hall within reach of those traveling the interstate, staff member Joe Ward says, "We hope there will be fewer winter days when we get only eight or ten people."

The uniforms, photographs, and famous-game basketballs are now shown in modern plexiglass display cases. The old hand-painted stained glass panels honoring individuals are gone, replaced by sculptured medallions in the new Court of Honor on the museum's third floor.

But many visitors might have trouble making it past the first floor, especially the person who can't walk past a schoolyard game without feeling the urge to step in and toss a few baskets.

The area is called "Shoot-Out," where visitors stand on a moving sidewalk and toss basketballs towards a bumper crop of baskets—close by, far away and in between. You will probably get off three or four shots before reaching the end of the conveyer, but you can walk through the turnstiles and wait for your turn to make free throws all over again. The child in each of us can't resist.

This participatory exhibit is as typical of the new hall as static display cases were of the old one. "Hoopla" is the name of a 35-millimeter film similar to those you may have seen at places like Epcot Center in Florida, or the Air and Space Museum at the Smithsonian Institution in Washington, D.C. A multitude of images is simultaneously featured on all parts of the huge screen as brilliant cinematography keeps your attention. (An opening panoramic aerial shot of a Rocky Mountain winter wonderland makes you feel as if you are in the National Skiing Hall of Fame.)

What do snow-packed mountains have to do with basketball? The message of "Hoopla" is that basketball is a true American sport, and the film may come close to convincing you that neither baseball nor football is qualified to be the national pastime. In the film, you see basketball backboards on big city playgrounds and on farms in the wheat fields of middle America. You see them at ocean-side parks and in high school gymnasiums all over the map. And amid the Colorado Rockies, after the introductory panorama, we see a small boy put on his boots and coat, trudge through newly-fallen snow, and shovel a path to his basketball net to practice layups.

"Hoopla" emphasizes amateur basketball over the NBA. But you can see memorable NBA as well as NCAA highlights with a push of a button at a number of video monitors. At one video screen, selections include: the Indiana State—Michigan State NCAA final game of 1979, with Larry Bird and Magic Johnson; the UCLA—Houston game played in the Astrodome before basketball's largest crowd; and a matchup between the Boston Celtics and the Los Angeles Lakers on January 18, 1981, again highlighting Bird and Johnson.

Watching these and similarly memorable moments brings back thoughts of where you were and what you were doing during important games, such as when Notre Dame ended UCLA's 88-game winning streak. You recall much more, as well as learn about basketball's history while walking through the displays next to the Court of Honor. One surprise was to see baseball Hall of Famers Lou Boudreau and Springfield's own Rabbit Maranville in basketball team photos before they embarked on their baseball careers. (You can assume that Maranville's 5-foot 5-inch height had something to do with his decision to leave the hoop sport.)

Classic college team photos offer proof of the quick acceptance of basketball fairly soon after Naismith developed it. There is the Dartmouth College men's team of 1909, the Vassar College women's team of 1907, and the Smith College women's team which played its first game on March 21, 1893, only two years after Naismith nailed two peach baskets to the walls. Incidentally, because the Smith women wore bloomers, no men were permitted to watch the game.

Women's contributions to basketball are fully recognized in the museum, and range from action shots in "Hoopla" to the honorees inducted into the hall; the first were honored in 1985, and the list consisted of:

coach Bertha Teague, player and coach Margaret Wade, and organizer of the first women's game at Smith, Senda Berenson Abbott.

These names may not be familiar to you, but, similarly, many names of male members of the Court of Honor ring a bell only to basketball diehards. Quite a few were contributors (Ralph Morgan and Oswald Tower, for example), or very early stars (such as Vic Hanson and Charles "Stretch" Murphy). Furthermore, this Hall of Fame is unique in that contributors and referees as well as players—high school and college along with professional—have a place here, too.

Location: The Naismith Memorial Basketball Hall of Fame is at 1150 West Columbus Avenue in Springfield. Traveling north, take exit 4 off Interstate 91 and follow the signs; travelling south along Interstate 91, take exit 7 and follow the signs; if you are coming from the Massachusetts Turnpike or Interstate 291, take exit 5 and follow the signs. **Admission** is charged. **Hours:** Daily, year round. **Allow** an hour and a half to three hours; diehards will want to spend significantly more time than casual fans. **Information:** Naismith Memorial Basketball Hall of Fame, 1150 West Columbus Avenue, P.O. Box 179, Springfield, MA 01101; (413) 781-6500.

INTERNATIONAL TENNIS HALL OF FAME

"The Sporting Lady of Bellevue Avenue," less romantically known as the Newport Casino, is the home of the International Tennis Hall of Fame.

FIRST OF ALL, LET'S MAKE THIS CLEAR: YOU DON'T HAVE TO BE A TENNIS aficionado to enjoy a visit to the International Tennis Hall of Fame.

This writer has been known to raise a racquet now and then, but well over half the names of the athletes enshrined in the hall mean little if anything to him.

Face it. How many of these do you recognize? Theodore R. Pell, Fred B. Alexander, Holcombe Ward, Harold H. Hackett, Marie Wagner.

But, like the Naismith Memorial Basketball Hall of Fame and many others, the enshrinees are not necessarily the prime lures. So what if you don't go back any further than Billie Jean King and John Newcombe?

You can still admire the evolution of tennis fashions, the sparkling assortment of trophies, and an architectural gem of a building.

The most sensational work of art may be the actual building which houses the hall and museum. Known for over a century as the Newport Casino, it sits across from a modern and nondescript shopping center and looks curious, but similarly unspectacular, from the Bellevue Avenue sidewalk that passes in front of it.

But after you pay your admission and enter the grounds, you are transported into the time of the Gilded Age when a Harvard education and smooth fitting tennis whites were prerequisites to participation in the game. There are turrets and towers, dark green trim on the Casino exterior and tennis green under the courtyard nets where the game is played regularly.

Gilded-age architects supreme McKim, Mead and White, who designed many of Newport's beautiful mansions, are also responsible for the Casino. Today, it looks much as it did on that hot summer day in 1880 when it first opened its doors.

The Newport Casino is the oldest, continuously used, tennis tournament site in the world. What about Wimbledon? It opened in 1877 but was rebuilt in 1922.

The U.S. National Championship, now the U.S. Open, wasn't always held in Forest Hills. The first U.S. Championship was at the Newport Casino, in 1881, and was won by Richard D. Sears. After taking top honors in the first U.S. Championship, Sears went on to win the next six. The U.S. Championship moved to Queens in 1915, in search of the bigger crowds New York City could provide.

Quite apart from the U.S. Championship, the Casino has been host to tournaments even since it first opened. (Only in the war years of 1917–1918, 1943–1945 were such events scrubbed.) The grand building is still, as sportswriter Bud Collins called it, "the sporting lady of Bellevue Avenue."

Today, the Casino is the site of the only professional tennis tournaments on grass in the United States: the Miller Lite/Hall of Fame Championships and the Virginia Slims Competition of Newport. The Casino is also notable for maintaining the only grass courts in the country open to the public for play. There is a fee and appointments are necessary.

The Hall of Fame itself is open in all four seasons and draws 70,000 annually. One of our favorite exhibits reflects the mood of the Casino's early days: the Casino Card Room has been restored to its 1885 appearance, complete with original tables and chairs. After looking at an appropriate setting from a century ago, stroll down the hall to glance at playing fashions of the time.

A more active display focusing on women in the sport can be found in the section appropriately titled "The Women in Tennis Room." The story is told through photographs and illustrations beginning with Gay '90s ladies like Bertha Townsend and Ellen Hansell and concluding with today's rising stars, including Andrea Jaeger of the United States, Claudia Kohde of West Germany and Hana Mandlikova of Czechoslovakia.

Like athletes and fashions, equipment has matured through the years. Admire the rows of racquets hanging on one gallery wall, and notice the worn and weary brown tennis shoes once donned by tennis pioneers. Then do a double-take at the early mold used to shape racquet frames in the 1870s. It looks like some kind of medieval torture instrument, or the handiwork of a depraved villain in a mad slasher movie.

In the last few years, the museum has placed a major emphasis on changing exhibits on numerous themes with one thing in common: a connection with tennis. For example, there have been displays on the development of tennis equipment, the Davis Cup, the International Lawn Tennis Clubs, women in tennis, court tennis, and the Grand Slam.

Although many of the names are unfamiliar to most casual visitors, one is drawn to the biographical sketches of those who belong to the Hall of Fame. They are divided chronologically into four sections: The Beginnings, 1873–1916; The Golden Age, 1917–1946; The Growth of Professionalism, 1947–1967; and The Open Era, 1968–present. Even if the names in the latter group are the only ones to which you can relate, you learn quite a bit about the game and its early heroes by reading about the others. But allow the time to do so; there are well over 150 tennis greats in the Hall of Fame.

Location: The International Tennis Hall of Fame is at 194 Bellevue Avenue in Newport near the corner of Memorial Boulevard and Bellevue. **Admission** is charged. **Hours:** Daily, year round. **Allow** one to two hours. **Information:** The International Tennis Hall of Fame, 194 Bellevue Avenue, Newport, RI 02840; (401) 849-3990.

NEW ENGLAND SKI MUSEUM

Can you remember when skis were made of wood? Only wood? These and others
are displayed in the New England Ski Museum.

F ACT: WHAT IS REGARDED AS THE OLDEST SKI CLUB IN THE COUNTRY
was founded over 100 years ago in Berlin, New Hampshire.

Fact: The first rope tow in America pulled anxious skiers up a Woodstock, Vermont, hill over 50 years ago.

Fact: The first T-Bar was established in 1940 at the Pico Peak ski area
in Vermont.

Theory: The slopes of New England produce better all-around skiers
than do the slopes out West.

Penny Pitou, at least, believes this theory. The Gilford, New Hampshire, native who won two silver medals in the 1960 Winter Olympics
says that skiers in New England, having to work under tough conditions,
learn how to handle themselves on ice, in winds, and in all sorts of other
unfavorable circumstances.

In addition, she reports, our ski areas are in close proximity to our
cities. Many assume that Denver, Colorado, is in the mountains; in reality,
it is situated in the plains at the eastern base of the Rockies. Penny, now

a travel agent in Laconia, New Hampshire, points out that Denver is two hours from the nearest major ski area and is a staggering five hours from the celebrated resort town of Aspen. By contrast, the millions of people in the New York, New Haven, Hartford-Springfield, and Boston metropolitan areas are within an hour or a bit longer from an abundance of top-notch New England ski centers.

So, taking into account our firsts in the world of skiing and the many superb skiers we have spawned, it is only fitting that New England should have created its own monument to the world's favorite winter sport. Ski buffs thought so, too, and in 1977 an organization was founded which began collecting ski memorabilia with the intention of exhibiting it to the public.

The vision was realized in Decmber 1982 when the New England Ski Museum in Franconia, New Hampshire, opened. Located in a former vehicle maintenance building adjacent to Cannon Mountain, the museum preserves and promotes New England's skiing heritage. Its geographical coverage extends beyond our six-state region, however, when required.

For example, one exhibit is focused on ski technique and instruction. To convey the proper background, visitors are introduced to Norway; evidence suggests that the first organized ski teaching was developed by the Norwegian military. They had troops on skis in the early 18th century, and many early ski instructors were military personnel, drill sergeants of the slopes. One illustration features a Scandinavian man wearing a short "pusher" ski on one shoe and a long "glider" ski on the other.

That sketch may not be on view when you visit: because of the museum's cozy quarters and vast archives in storage, executive director Linda Gray says that most of the exhibits will change annually. "We only have room for so much, and we have large collections of black and white photographs and memorabilia that we want to show."

Certain artifacts and features are permanent, however. One is an ongoing program of vintage videos from the museum's archives. Visitors can watch past Olympic games, "Legends of American Skiing," and other classic portrayals of skiers on film.

Skiing history continues, featuring Brattleboro, Vermont native Fred Harris and his creation in 1909 of the Dartmouth Outing Club, which sponsors the classic Dartmouth Winter Carnival, still going strong well into its eighth decade. In the 1940s, soldiers crossed the Alps on skis during World War II, while on the home front, express trains with names like the Ski Meister and the Eastern Snow Express made direct excursions to New Hampshire's mountains before the days of major interstates and all-weather tires.

The equipment that skiers carried on those trains stands in a silent tribute to Yankee ingenuity. Crude wooden skis were developed first;

aluminum and, in the 1970s, fiberglass gradually replaced hickory. Primitive poles with leather lacing, experimental model skis, and old boots that predate the 1932 Lake Placid Winter Olympics indicate the changes made in the ski industry in a little over half a century.

Location: The New England Ski Museum is at Parkway exit 2, next to the Cannon Mountain tram. **Admission** is free. **Hours:** Daily except Wednesday, late May through mid-October, and late December through late March. **Allow** a half hour. **Information:** The New England Ski Museum, P.O. Box 267, Franconia, NH 03580; (603) 823-7177.

NEW ENGLAND SPORTS MUSEUM

This life-size sculpture of Bobby Orr, carved from a 2,200-pound block of basswood over the course of about 2,000 hours, was created for the Sports Museum of New England by Armand LaMontaigne.

IF YOU HAD A CHOICE, WHICH OF THE FOLLOWING WOULD YOU NAME as your all-time favorite moment in New England sports history:

Dave Henderson's improbable home run against the California Angels in the 1986 baseball playoffs?

Doug Flutie's last-second "Hail Mary" touchdown pass against the University of Miami in 1984?

The incredible comeback of 16 points in 42 seconds by Harvard to tie Yale in their 1968 football game?

Joan Benoit's arduous victory in the 1984 Olympics?

All can be relived on videotape in the New England Sports Museum in Cambridge, Massachusetts. The museum, located for five years on Soldier's Field Road in nearby Allston, relocated to CambridgeSide Galleria in the spring of 1993.

Sit yourself down in one of several small theaters in this tribute to New England sports and watch the legends bat, run, kick, and slam dunk once more. Or examine a baseball bat used in the 1903 World Series by Fred Parent of the Boston Pilgrims (later the Red Sox). Then have your picture taken next to a six-foot-round bowling ball, looking like a refugee from the Jolly Green Giant's candlepin alley.

Why did the museum move from Allston to Cambridge? There are many reasons, and size is the biggest. The old museum in Allston was cramped, providing only 2,500 square feet of exhibit space. Once could peruse the displays in a half hour or less. The new museum is over six times that size with room for permanent visual and auditory tributes to all major New England sports, and some minor ones as well.

In addition, the Soldiers Field Road location was out of the way, entrenched in a nondescript building in Christian Herter Park. It wasn't the kind of place people would stumble into serendipitously, and consequently it drew only 15,000 to 20,000 people per year. The museum staff is hoping for upwards of 200,000 visitors per year in the new locale, which has easy access to mass transit and is within 200 yards of the Museum of Science.

Museum Development Assistant Jeff Jackson admits, however, that "the idea of going into a mall is kind of weird for a museum." But the tons of foot traffic—about four million people per year step inside the mall, Jackson estimates—and therefore many spur-of-the-moment visitors is a boon. The CambridgeSide Galleria became the museum's home thanks to the friendship of mall owners Dave Cowens, former Boston Celtics star and Sports Museum chairman, and Stephen Karp, the chief executive officer of New England Development.

Perhaps the most eye-catching exhibits in the museum are three true works of art—life-sized wooden sculptures of Larry Bird, Bobby Orr, and

Carl Yastrzemski. All are the products of the skilled hands of Rhode Island artist Armand LaMontagne and are incredibly lifelike.

Put your own hands in the place of Tony Pena's when you try to catch a Roger Clemens fast ball in a special exhibit that simulates being on the receiving end of the Rocket's pitching arm. "Catching Clemens" is incorporated into the baseball gallery, which includes many appropriate motifs such as bat columns holding up light fixtures shaped like baseballs, and light sconces in the shape of baseball diamonds. And your feet walk on green carpet, evocative of a baseball outfield.

The video theater in the baseball gallery comes replete with about a dozen Fenway Park seats for viewing nearly a century of Boston professional baseball highlights. The theater's exterior has been painted to resemble Fenway's outside. Other theaters in the museum resemble the exteriors of Boston Garden and Harvard Stadium.

From the beginning, Dick Johnson said the museum's concept would be to include all New England sports, participatory as well as professional. So it is only natural that our only true regional sport is featured in a gallery of its own. A trio of candlepins taller than Robert Parish on stilts sums up New Englanders' affection for their own brand of bowling.

Spare us, you say? Strike that thought. Other features of the candlepin exhibit include a working pin setter, a word wall of bowling terms and a six-foot-round bowling ball containing the name and location of every candlepin bowling center in New England.

Even the lobby is vibrant. It is home to the New England Sports Wall, consisting of separate 24 by 30 inch color transparencies mounted on a grid with front access, and rear illuminated with fluorescent light strips. And don't let anyone tell you that you are too small to play sports. Another wall display is titled, "Champions Come in All Sizes." In front of an eight-foot-high freestanding wall are full scale photographs of sports figures mounted on cut-outs. You can compare your stature to that of athletes like Parish, figure skater Nancy Kerrigan, and jockey Chris McCarron.

And to tease your mind, you will undoubtedly discover a cache of trivia upon your visit. For example, anyone who remembers LBJ, Sergeant Pepper, and Jim Lonborg will gravitate towards the exhibit on the 1967 World Series. And can you recall who started the must-win sixth Series game for the Sox? Hint: he was a native of Connecticut and was barely in the majors long enough for a cup of coffee before being called on to pitch in that crucial game.

Give up? It was Gary Waslewski, who would go on to play with five teams in a six-year career, retiring with a lifetime won-lost record of 11–26. He did the job that October day, however, ensuring himself a place in baseball annals by limiting the Cardinals to four hits and two runs in five and one third innings in a game the Red Sox would win, 8–4.

Location: By MBTA, take the Green Line to Lechmere. From Interstate 93, take the Storrow Drive exit. Then take the first exit to Cambridge and follow the signs to the Museum of Science. The museum is one block west of the Museum of Science. **Admission** is charged. **Hours:** Year-round, daily. **Allow** an hour and a half. **Information:** The Sports Museum of New England, CambridgeSide Galleria, 100 CambridgeSide Place, Suite #133, Cambridge, MA 02151; (617) 57-SPORT [(617) 577-7678].

SHELBURNE MUSEUM

Courtesy: Shelburne Museum

All dolled up for a night on the town is this early American quartet, part of Shelburne Museum's huge doll collection.

THERE IS A CRAZY QUILT HANGING IN THE HAT AND FRAGRANCE SHOP at the Shelburne Museum in Shelburne, Vermont. It dazzles and it overwhelms. You don't know where to look first.

The quilt is a metaphor for the Shelburne Museum, a massive complex whose name is a blatant misnomer. This is a museum like the Taj Mahal is a bungalow.

There are 37 exhibit buildings, with the word "building" meaning anything from the reproduction of a New York Park Avenue luxury apartment to a historic, turn-of-the-century side-wheeler steamboat that is literally in drydock. And like the crazy quilt, which is one of 200,000 objects to be seen, Shelburne Museum is as dazzling as it is overwhelming.

"Playthings" abound: dolls, toys, decoys, and many other objects which, by a very loose definition, can also fit the category, not all of which were meant to be used by children for their amusement.

The Shelburne Toy Shop is the best place to see antique trains, penny banks, music boxes, toy boats and dolls. Some toys served educational purposes long before "Sesame Street." A wooden knock-down doll can be taken apart and reassembled, but only a child with a great deal of patience and skill can manage the feat. For the religious who considered idle playtime to be sinful, there was a little Noah's Ark with miniature twosomes of all the animals that took the cruise with Noah and survived the great flood.

You can spend the better part of a morning or afternoon just studying the dolls, which come in every conceivable image, from a medieval court jester to Shirley Temple. The collection of 18th) and 19th-century dolls is extensive, and includes stuffed homespun dolls, porcelain dolls, wooden dolls, papier-mâché dolls, leather dolls and apple-head dolls. A 19th-century fisherman with rain slicker and hat looks as if he just stepped off a boat at Gloucester. An unlikely counterpart is the elegant 19th-century French fashion doll in her long Parisian gown. "Aunt Peggy," a 19th-century wooden doll, looks the part of the clichéd American homebody.

Like some toys, dolls were also used for purposes other than play. Some, like Indian dolls, had a deep religious significance; others, such as the French fashion doll, were used as an advertising gimmick to lure customers.

Then there are the toys for adults. Vermont Governor Edward C. Smith had his own private railroad car. It was called the "Grande Isle," dates from the 1890s, and is on view at Shelburne as a symbol of the fabled era of railroading. It boasts mahogany panelling and velvet furnishings throughout its seven rooms. Private railroad cars were out of the reach of the average citizen, but popular among the rich and famous of the period. The "Grande Isle" is a grand example and is on the must-see list of all visiting railroad buffs.

All visitors have special interests and, therefore, their own favorites. We had two. One was the Variety Unit, with its collections of toby jugs, scrimshaw, matchboxes, blown glass rolling pins, dollhouses, Victorian-era Valentine's Day cards and so on. The collections of playthings, ornaments, and show pieces in this one building are simply endless.

Our other favorite was the Stagecoach Inn, which we loved for its diverse examples of New England folk art, some of which were once practical and now are used to gracefully decorate. Eagles that once

Courtesy: Shelburne Museum

Patterns that look like a kaleidoscope gone crazy are found in Shelburne's quilt exhibits.

adorned our region's colonial houses roost proudly, while wooden figure-heads seem to look in wonder as to what happened to the rest of their ships.

Trade signs and sculptures of wood are exhibited here, too. Among others, there is a mortar and pestle which once hung from an apothecary shop; a pineapple, the age-old symbol of hospitality; a chubby Jack Tar, which served to identify a 19th-century ship chandlery; and a late 19th-century sculpted figure of the minstrel show character Jim Crow, which had been propped in front of a cigar store. (The Jim Crow figure, racist by today's standards, was a not-so-uncommon sight 100 years ago, proof that the good old days weren't good for all.)

For those whose interests stretch beyond toys, dolls, and folk art, there are a number of colonial and other old houses moved here over the years. (The properly named Stencil House is worth a stop just to see its wonderfully stencilled walls.) More than 1,000 early wild fowl decoys can be seen in the Dorset House. The nostalgia-minded trot over to the Horseshoe Barn to inspect, in what seems like a Currier and Ives lithograph that has come to life, 100 antique carriages, coaches and sleighs, some imported from Paris for the fashionable Webb family, whose descendants founded the museum.

Unlike a church steeple or a widow's walk that might pierce the skyline at many similar early New England villages, at Shelburne it's the land-locked boat, S.S. *Ticonderoga*, that commands attention. The *Ti*, quite possibly the favorite attraction of most visitors, sailed the waters of Lake Champlain from 1906 to 1953. When you hop on board today, you can see the boat's inner workings, the red dining room carpeting, typical cabins, the green velvet chairs, and a short film which, while somewhat dated, is a fascinating record of the boat's arduous, two-mile overland move from the lake to Shelburne.

Location: To reach Shelburne Museum, take Interstate 89 north to Interstate 189 in Burlington to Route 7 south to the museum. **Admission** is charged. **Hours:** Daily, late May through late October; single, daily guided tour the rest of the year. **Allow** at least four hours. **Information:** Shelburne Museum, Shelburne, VT 05482; (802) 985-3344. **Note:** You would need at least two days to see everything the Shelburne Museum has to offer. But it is easy to suffer from burnout, and a stay of five or six hours seems optimum. The best plan upon reaching Shelburne is to take a few minutes to look over the free guide map and decide which attractions interest you most before seeing anything. You are allowed free admission for a second day with your ticket in peak season.

THE COMPUTER MUSEUM

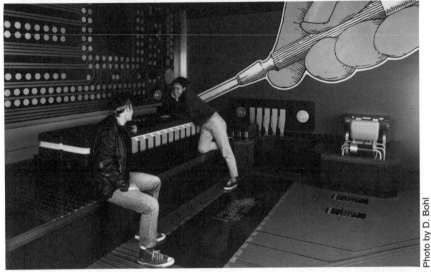

"A playground for the mind" is the way one visitor described The Computer Museum.

Y AWN.

I was on my way to a computer museum.

Computers and I have never had a placid relationship. For a long time we had no relationship at all. It took ages for me to buy a word processor and for years I did my writing on a clunky portable Smith-Corona typewriter that was a broken-down lemon since the day I took it home. Doing simple arithmetic on a pocket calculator had long been the extent of my computer experience.

I didn't care that this Boston site, opened in November 1984, was the only computer museum in the world. I expected it to be a pretty dry place with technical exhibits and a lot of guys walking around looking just like the kids in school we called Poindexter—the ones who carried slide rules as extensions of their arms.

I heard a visitor who entered the museum in front of me, obviously no stranger to it, say to his compatriot, "This place is a playground for the mind."

Maybe to him it is. I looked for his slide rule, but he must have had it concealed in his winter coat.

We rode in an elevator the size of a truck—this converted warehouse at Museum Wharf previously housed a major transportation museum—to the sixth floor, where the museum begins; I was ready to be bored.

But I wasn't ready for what I would find.

Nobody—and I mean nobody, no matter how computer illiterate he or she is—can not be awestruck when first sighting the biggest working computer in the world. It is two stories high and has a 25-foot wide keyboard. The rotund rolling trackball, over three feet in diameter, guides the cursor along a monitor as big as the north wall in a suburban master bedroom.

And yes, it is fully operative. I waited my turn, then had this behemoth of computers figure the shortest distance between New York and Sydney, as well as several other cities, as the computer flashed images of city landmarks on the massive monitor.

I then took the guided tour through the inside of the Walk-Through Computer, sort of a technical Fantastic Voyage. I didn't understand every techno-term our guide used but I did see for myself that it is not magic that makes these things run. The world's largest microchips (sounds sort of like "giant pygmies" or "jumbo shrimp") and the 15-foot hard disk drive help put things in perspective.

Of course, the museum had some boring parts I expected to find. I read about core memory simulation—understood little of it—and slept through a five-minute edited film clip from a 1963 U.S. Air Force promotional film on the Q–7 computer and its role in the SAGE (Semi-Automatic Ground Environment System) air defense system.

Ho-hum.

But as I walked through the many galleries here, I continued to amaze myself. In an exhibit titled "People and Computers," which showcases the effect computer technology has had on human culture and history, I took in a bit of nostalgia. A videotape of election night 1952 features CBS newscasters Walter Cronkite and Charles Collingwood trying to coax voting totals from a UNIVAC computer. (Remember the UNIVAC? Its name was an acronym for Universal Automatic Computer.) "You're a very impolite machine, I must say," said a scorned Collingwood when UNIVAC initially would not spew out results on cue.

Another video accompanies Whirlwind, a one-of-a-kind Neanderthal developed across the river at the Massachusetts Institute of Technology in 1952. Featured on tape here is a December 1952 segment of the old CBS show, "See It Now," in which host Edward R. Murrow conducts an interview with the still-in-diapers Whirlwind.

I watched as Whirlwind first calculated how long a rocket would take to use up its fuel. Murrow was as lost as I was with the answer, so he asked Whirlwind a less complex question: if the Indians had invested the $24 they received for purchasing Manhattan Island at an interest rate of 6%, how much would they have today?

Whirlwind calculated that in 1751, they would have had $34,949. In 1951, their fortune would have totaled $4,027,727,969. Whirlwind then stepped into the deep, dark future, figuring that in the far-off year of 1985, the Indians who traded Manhattan would have earned $29,175,403,543. For its encore, Whirlwind played "Jingle Bells" in what must have been the first time millions of Americans would hear a computer play a song.

They still play music, I was about to learn. In one of over 125 interactive exhibits, a computer and I were able to utilize the sounds of drumsticks and keyboards to play some deep fried Memphis blues.

This was getting fun, I thought. Apprehensive at first, I parked myself down in front of a computer in a gallery called Tools and Toys and figured out the ideal wine to serve with a dinner of chateaubriand (a dry, light-bodied, red wine called Valpolicello).

It was easy. At another computer I bargained with a fruit vendor, like the ones at Boston's Haymarket Square. At another, I designed a deck, then saw how computers design running shoes.

I couldn't wait to try another. I sat at yet another that played word games. The computer gave me and my (human) companion a list of words—we picked "children"—and we had to make as many smaller words as we could from the letters in it. We (the humans) played against each other and were awarded points for each word. The computer even served up bonus points for defining some of the words.

We came up with 50 words and were quite proud of them: "lichen," "niche," and "chide," for example. The computer was happy to show us another 45 we missed; its list included "nide," "ceil," and "elhi." I learned a few new words. This was starting to be fun.

In a gallery devoted to graphics, I played color by number, and then watched a digital typographer color and shade an instant photograph of me. I spoke into a handset to see sound frequencies displayed on an oscilloscope screen, and examined computer-enhanced digital photographs of the Shroud of Turin.

I was wishing I had allowed more time for my visit. I had only a few moments to gaze at the exhibit on robots and to interact with HAL, a video exhibit based on the movie 2001: A Space Odyssey.

Before I left, I stopped to peek inside the first floor gift shop. Along with games, posters, jewelry, postcards, and an edible chocolate "chip," was a book that three hours earlier would have interested me. It was titled "The Unofficial I Hate Computers Book." But after my stay here, I simply couldn't fit into the category of a computer hater anymore. And I can't wait to spring the word "nide" on unsuspecting opponents next time we play Scrabble.

Location: The Computer Museum is at Museum Wharf in Boston. By MBTA, take Red Line to South Station and walk across the Congress Street bridge. By car, from the south, take Interstate 93 to the Downtown–Mass. Pike–Chinatown exit. Bear left to sign marked "Downtown Boston." At the end of the ramp, take a right onto Kneeland Street to South Station. Then go left onto Atlantic Avenue, go through two lights, right on Congress Street and across bridge. From the north, take Interstate 93 to exit 23 (High and Congress Streets). Take the first left onto Congress Street and cross the bridge. From the west, take the Mass. Pike (Interstate 90) to Downtown Boston, South Station exit. Go through three lights onto Congress Street and cross the bridge. **Admission** is charged. **Hours:** Year-round, daily in summer; closed Monday the rest of the year; half price admission Sunday late afternoons. **Information:** The Computer Museum, Museum Wharf, 300 Congress Street, Boston, MA 02210; (617) 423-6758 for recorded information and events listing; (617) 426-2800 for museum offices. **Note:** Paid parking is available in private lots on Congress Street past the museum. Museum Wharf is marked by a huge artificial milk bottle, once the property of the Hood Milk Company.

BARNUM MUSEUM AND NEW ENGLAND CAROUSEL MUSEUM

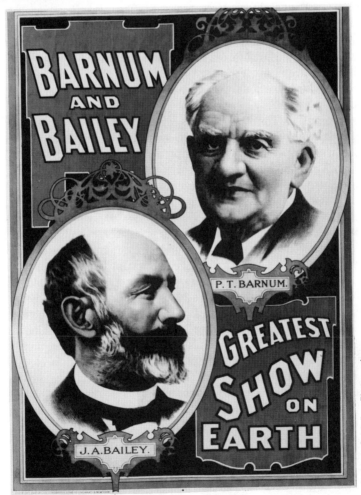

This 1897 advertising poster for Barnum and Bailey's "Greatest Show on Earth" is among the circus memorabilia on view at the Barnum Museum in Bridgeport, Connecticut.

IF YOU'D LIKE, JUST ONCE IN YOUR LIFE, TO JOURNEY BACK TO CHILD-hood—those hobby horse days of cotton candy and carousels—head to the state of Connecticut where you will have the opportunity to do so twice. Two museums—one opened in 1989, the other refurbished and reopened in 1989—are waiting to transport you back to the days of your earliest memories.

The first, in Bridgeport, is the Barnum Museum which is certain to trigger happy memories in anyone who has been thrilled by the sight of airborne acrobats and obedient elephants. The second, in Bristol, is the New England Carousel Museum where a menagerie of hand carved and gilded, horses, lions, and dragons are lovingly restored and displayed.

Visitors to the Barnum Museum are surrounded by the sights and sounds of the circus as they enter the world of the professional performers who achieved international recognition as stars of P.T. Barnum's "Greatest Show on Earth."

The diminutive Tom Thumb, his wife Lavinia Warren, and ex-slave Joice Heth, were among the best known members of Barnum's troupe. Barnum was responsible for bringing Jenny Lind, the Swedish Night-ingale, to America. Upon her arrival, Lindmania swept the country. The Barnum Museum's collections of Jenny Lind bonnets, Jenny Lind shawls, Jenny Lind riding hats, and Jenny Lind gloves bear testimony to the appeal of this singer.

First and foremost, Barnum was a promoter. Though he is widely associated with the circus that bears his name, many people are surprised to learn that he didn't organize his first circus until he was over 60. Earlier in life, Barnum founded two museums in New York City, exploiting both the weird and the wonderful. He also served as mayor of Bridgeport, and was a fervent abolitionist; as a member of the Connecticut state legislature, he voted to ratify the 14th Amendment, abolishing slavery.

The museum's first floor focuses on Barnum the person, and through a variety of media, the visitor is introduced to this multi-faceted man. In fact, Barnum introduces himself in the form of a talking, six-foot-tall, animated mannequin. He rightly claims that he "made a bit of a profit" over the sixty years he "dazzled the nation with curiosities and marvels unmatched in the history of humankind."

Barnum entered the business of doing pleasure when he presented to the public Joice Heth, a former slave who claimed to be 161 years old. After her death, an autopsy showed her to be no more than 80, causing Barnum to admit, "the bigger the humbug, the better the people like it."

Other points of interest on the first floor include the zoetropes and praxinoscopes, Victorian era mechanical toys, circular in shape that spin still images (photographs or silk paintings) over a light source to produce moving images of acrobats on horseback, dogs jumping through hoops, and clowns juggling.

The second floor centers on Barnum and his relationship with his home city. Barnum the showman is celebrated on the third floor. Though his circus dominates the exhibits, the visitor is also introduced to his museums, where Bridgeport's most famous son first gained recognition as a huckster and promoter.

Despite his penchant for the tawdry and sensational, Barnum was a bona fide promoter of the arts. He introduced the Punch and Judy Show to American audiences and often presented legitimate theater in his New York museums.

The third floor gallery, the museum's largest, houses a hand-carved miniature circus that occupies 1,000 square feet and contains over 3,000 figures (many of them animated), including: animals and performers, carpenters and cooks, boxcars, wagons, and an admiring audience.

Surrounding the miniature circus is an elevated viewing ramp dotted with miniature video monitors which display vintage big top highlights, and commentaries on circus life. Among circus employees there was a strict pecking order. A partition in the dining tent separated workmen from the performers and the business staff; among performers, riders were the elite and sat at the head of the table.

A circus without clowns is like carbonated soda without fizz. Spend some time admiring the tools of the clown's trade: baggy pants, obtrusive hats, stilts, a bass drum bearing a picture of a wart-faced old hag labeled, "my mother-in-law" and a gigantic bra that even Dolly Parton could swim in. There are also mirrors marked with vibrant make-up, so you can see what you'd look like dressed for success as a clown.

If, after having seen the circus, you are still reluctant to return to the present, the charms (and artistry) of the past era are in profusion at the New England Carousel Museum, only forty miles from the Barnum Museum, in Bristol, Connecticut.

No one can keep from smiling upon entering the Carousel Museum. Herds of horses, prides of lions, and creatures of pure fancy, in all their hand-carved, gilded diversity will delight the eye and soothe the spirit of any visitor from the late twentieth century.

Once past the initial enchantment, visitors can appreciate the skill and labor of the individual artists—the majority of whom were immigrants from Europe who brought their training with them.

A recreated workshop invites the visitor into the carousel artist's world. Since many of these workers hadn't mastered English, they communicated their plans and ideas by drawing them on a wall-length canvas that was, perhaps, the most important of all of the turn-of-the-century tools in the workshop's collection.

The people behind the Carousel Museum are Bill Finkenstein and his wife Claudia, who refurbish antique carousel animals and chariots as R&F Designs, Inc. Finkenstein notes that the same artists whose work was rather subdued when completed in Germany "flourished after they came to the United States."

Though a craftsman couldn't sign his creation, he found other ways of leaving his mark. The preeminent German craftsman, Marcus Charles Illions, carved horses with faces resembling deer. Another artist depicted his equines with long snouts and fierce or sad faces. A third producer of carousel animals, the Philadelphia Toboggan Company, always provided its stallions with square saddles.

Many of the creatures are R&F Design projects and, once restored, are sent home to the parks and playgrounds where they will be ridden by people of all ages. Bill's handiwork can be seen nearby, at Lake Compounce amusement park in Bristol, or as far away as the City Park carousel in New Orleans.

There is more. The visitor will hear Wurlitzer band organs, with their brassy drums and crashing cymbals, and gaze at the mural by artist Cortlandt Hull which depicts a fantasy gathering at Santa Monica Pier of old-time movie stars whose careers coincided with the golden years of the carousel.

Location: The Barnum Museum is at 820 Main Street, Bridgeport. From Interstate 95 south, take exit 27 and bear right following the sign for Lafayette Boulevard. Follow onto Lafayette, turn right onto State Street, then right onto Main Street. From Interstate 95 north, take exit 27 and continue straight off the exit ramp through four lights, then turn left at the fifth light onto Main Street. On weekends, street parking is easy to find. On weekdays, the best idea is to park at the Hi-Ho Garage on Lafayette Boulevard, two blocks away. **Admission** is charged. **Hours:** Year round, Tuesday through Saturday and Sunday afternoons. **Allow** an hour and a half to three hours. **Information:** The Barnum Museum, 820 Main Street, Bridgeport, CT 06604; (203) 331-1104.

Location: The New England Carousel Museum is at 95 Riverside Avenue (Route 72), Bristol. Take exit 31 off Interstate 84 (West Street). **Admission** is charged. **Hours:** Year round, Sunday through Friday afternoons, Saturday all day. **Allow** an hour for the tour. **Information:** The New England Carousel Museum, 95 Riverside Avenue, Bristol, CT 06010; (203) 585-5411. **Note:** If a visit here whets your appetite, keep in mind that you can ride on the Bushnell Park Carousel in downtown Hartford for 25 cents; (203) 728-3089.

MAINE TRANSPORTATION

The Red Baron demonstrates his World War I Fokker triplane at many of the summer and fall airshows at the Owls Head Transportation Museum.

Courtesy: Owls Head Transportation Museum

THE OBSOLETE HAS TREMENDOUS APPEAL. WHY ELSE WOULD PEOPLE take jet airplanes or drive their BMW's to places where they stand and look at the old-fashioned vehicles that moved us around decades ago?

Young people marvel at Model T's and open cockpit planes, and wonder how their grandparents coped with the unreliability and discomfort of these vehicles. Older folks look at these dinosaurs with fondness and often forget the inconvenience and occasional terrors that accompanied the use of early automobiles and flying machines.

The Maine coast is blessed with several museums devoted to the dawn of our modern era of transportation. The towns of Boothbay, Owls Head and Kennebunkport all greet the visitor with the shriek of steam whistles, the clang of electric trolley bells, and the slow flutter of wooden propellors.

Boothbay Railway Village introduces visitors to the time when the steam train was king. Several buildings form a representative village centered around a railroad station. Visitors may ride a steam-powered narrow gauge train and immerse themselves in railroad memorabilia. They may also visit the bank, the barber shop, and the hardware store as well as other public buildings typical of the time.

Boothbay's main train station came from Freeport, today the home of L.L. Bean and other factory outlets. When the station was built in 1911, however, Freeport was just one of many stops on the Maine Central Railroad. The Freeport station serves as a repository for old luggage, railroad spikes, menus, dining car table settings, a collection of photographs, and other artifacts of the heyday of the railroad industry. There is a second station, this one built circa 1870 on Maine's Belfast and Moosehead Lake Railroad line. Called Thorndike Station, it has a recreated railroad office.

Boothbay's narrow gauge railroad, the Boothbay Central, carries passengers one and a half times around the village. The end of the line is Summit Station where visitors may examine displays that answer questions about this particular narrow gauge railroad.

What is a narrow gauge railroad? The term "gauge" refers to the distance between the rails. Standard gauge tracks are four feet, eight inches apart, while any tracks that are closer together are considered to be narrow gauge. The Boothbay Central's tracks are two feet apart. During the height of the railroad era, there were more narrow gauge tracks in Maine than anywhere else in the country. The operating cost of the Boothbay Central's narrow gauge railroad was one fifth that of a standard gauge line.

Of course, when they weren't riding the railroad, local citizens could be found about town, perhaps in the general store. Remember boric acid and Bon Ami cleanser? They are still displayed in Dingley's Store, moved here from Waldoboro, Maine in 1969. There's a cornucopia of artificial produce like squash, grapes, green beans, corn, pineapples and oranges, and in the front window is a package for 1000 sheets of Morgan Wire Hook Boudoir Paper.

Local services are also represented. There's an open ledger dated 1893 at the tiny Canal Bank. Nearby is the Z.P. Merry barber shop, where many a Boothbay man had his hair clipped while talking sports and politics. Bottles of Wildroot and Vitalis occupy shelf space, while a sign posts haircut prices at five cents, neck shaves at ten cents and extravagant pompadour cuts at 100 cents.

Boothbay Railway Village also has an automobile collection. Many cars are on loan, so the display changes. On display when we visited was a 1911 Model T Ford delivery truck from Lydia E. Pinkham's Vegetable Compound, a 1946 cranberry red Volvo, a 1922 hearse, and a classic 1962

Nash Metropolitan. Accepted as the first American subcompact car, the Nash carried a $1,673 price tag.

As we were leaving, we heard a man say to his wife, "Don't tell me about the cars I should have saved, especially the ones that you had a lot to do with giving away."

He may find some of his old cars further north at the Owls Head Transportation Museum, just outside Rockland. Here is a mulligan stew of ancient cars, memorable airplanes, and antique bicycles.

The Owls Head Transportation Museum is well regarded for its special events scheduled on summer weekends. Events include meets for classic and antique Fords, Chevrolets, motorcycles, convertibles and trucks, and air shows spotlighting aircraft from both world wars.

The cream of summer events is the two-day rally and aerobatic show, in early August, with over 300 vehicles. There is a consolation prize for those who can't attend the event—a thirty minute videotape of the 1988 rally.

At Rockland's most unique parking lot—the hangar that's home for the museum's vehicles—there are aisles of autos with names you will recognize, such as Ford and Mercedes, and others, like Panhard Levassur, that long ago fell into obscurity. On most weekends, short rides in a Model T are offered on the museum's runway. Maine's own Stanley brothers are represented by three models of their famous Steamers. So is Sears Roebuck, which sold 3,500 of its own cars through its catalog.

One happy Sears customer in 1908 said, "It beats a horse bad, as it don't eat when it ain't working, and it stands without hitching and best of all, it don't get scared at automobiles."

He could have said the same about any of the Victorian era bicycles on exhibit, or the early motorcycles that are part of the collection. The Owls Head Transportation Museum also has a 1909 Bleriot Type X1 and other early aircraft. Construction machinery, such as a 1913 International Harvester tractor and a 1926 steam roller, is also on display.

Trolleys are even more of a site for nostalgic eyes, since they are as close to extinction as the California condor. When the conductor at the Seashore Trolley Museum in Kennebunkport calls out, "All aboard," you have a chance to take a ride on a real endangered species.

At one time, several of the museum's motormen had actually been trolleymen in their younger years. Says Museum Director Donald Curry, "As time passes, fewer and fewer remain. But we have a lot who rode trolleys as children and are now fulfilling a frustrated amibition they had as kids."

The 25-minute-long, bumpy ride along the museum's tracks takes you into the Maine woods while the conductor shares a bit of his knowledge. The first horse-drawn rail cars appeared in New York City in 1832, and by the Civil War they were transporting millions of people. Horses, costly to keep and susceptible to disease, couldn't be replaced until a young inventor named Frank Sprague perfected the electric streetcar. The trolley gave birth to the suburbs in the early 20th century.

A perennial favorite of visitors here is the classy "City of Manchester" parlor car, not a typical trolley, but a true work of art with its velvet drapes, wicker chairs, leather seats, and liquor cabinets. It was used to cart dignitaries around the New Hampshire city in the days when both automobiles and baseball were still young.

Baseball's growing popularity coincided with increased ridership on trolleys. There were so many trolleys in Brooklyn, New York, that the borough named its National League baseball team the Trolley Dodgers, which eventually was shortened to the Dodgers. A red trolley with re-movable sides from Brooklyn is a relic of that time.

Not all the trolleys here are American. There is a strapping double decker from England, a stubby little car from Berlin, Germany, as well as others from Japan, Italy, and Canada. Montreal's open-topped "Golden Chariot" was a boon for summer sightseers, while the enclosed green heavyweight car from Montreal with its polished cherry wood and ornate brass light fixtures took commuters up and down Saint Catherine and other downtown streets for 43 years.

There are over 200 trolleys and other mass-transit vehicles of all shapes and sizes stored in the museum's four barns. It is hard to believe that when the museum was founded in 1939, it had just one trolley, an open car from the nearby Biddeford and Saco line which took summertime travelers to Old Orchard Beach. It is still on view today.

Location: Boothbay Railway Village is on Route 27 in Boothbay. **Admission** is charged. **Hours:** Mid-June to mid-October, daily. **Allow** two to two and a half hours. **Information:** Boothbay Railway Village, Box 123, Boothbay, ME 04537; (207) 633-4727. **Note:** There are a few picnic tables on the grounds and the gift shop has a substantial selection of books relating to railroads.

Location: The Owls Head Transportation Museum is on Route 73, two miles south of the center of Rockland. **Admission** is charged. **Hours:** Year-round, daily. **Allow** an hour, significantly more when special events are scheduled. **Information:** Owls Head Transportation Museum, P.O. Box 277, Owls Head, ME 04854; (207) 594-4418.

Location: The Seashore Trolley Museum is on Log Cabin Road in Kennebunkport. From the south, take Interstate 95, exit 3, onto Route 35 south, then Route 1 north for 2.8 miles, then right onto Log Cabin Road for 1.7 miles. From the north, take Interstate 95, exit 4. Continue straight ahead to Route 1. Turn right and follow Route 1 for about three miles to Log Cabin Road. Turn left on Log Cabin Road. **Admission** is charged. **Hours:** May through mid-October, daily; shorter hours spring and fall. **Allow** two hours. **Information:** Seashore Trolley Museum, P.O. Box A, Kennebunkport, ME 04046; (207) 967-2800.

Note: If you are hungry for more, consider visiting the Wells Auto Museum on Route 1 in Wells, home to 70 antique cars, mostly American made, and nickelodeons and picture machines; (207) 646-9064.

ADDITIONAL LISTINGS

Hᴇʀᴇ ᴀʀᴇ ᴏᴛʜᴇʀ ᴘʟᴀᴄᴇs ᴡʜᴇʀᴇ ʏᴏᴜ ᴄᴀɴ sᴇᴇ ᴄᴏʟʟᴇᴄᴛɪᴏɴs ᴏғ sports memorabilia, toys, dolls, games and other amusements.

Hartford, CT. Butler-McCook Homestead. Has collections of toys and dolls. Mid-May through mid-October. (203) 522-1806.

Wiscasset, ME. Musical Wonder House Music Museum. Memorial Day through mid-October. (800) 339-7163 (Maine), (800) 336-3725 (elsewhere).

Holyoke, MA. Volleyball Hall of Fame. Year-round. (413) 536-0926.

Sandwich, MA. Yesteryears Doll and Miniature Museum. Mid-May through mid-October. (508) 888-1711.

Wenham, MA. Wenham Historical Association and Museum. Has more than 5,000 dolls, dollhouses and toys. Year-round; closed in early February. (508) 468-2377.

Hampton, NH. Tuck Memorial Museum. Has old toys. Mid-June through mid-September. (603) 929-0781.

Portsmouth, RI. Green Animals. Museum of Victorian toys in main house. May through September; weekends in October. (401) 847-1000.

Newport, RI. Museum of Yachting. Mid-May through October. (401) 847-1018.

Manchester, VT. The American Museum of Fly-Fishing. Year-round. (802) 362-3300.

Woodstock, VT. Woodstock Historical Society's Dana House. Dolls, dollhouses, miniatures, toys; sleighs, sleds, early skis. May through October. (802) 457-1822.

OPEN ALL WINTER

OPEN ALL WINTER.

That's a phrase some might say we never hear in New England. But it's as false as the aluminum Christmas trees they buy in California.

Many of New England's most popular summer attractions are also open in colder weather. A wintertime visit allows you access to some of New England's most special places without the crowds, the waits, and the tour buses. You won't have to stand in line or trip over hordes of schoolchildren.

Then there's the guilt-trip.

Who hasn't had an experience like this in the summer? It is 85 degrees outside, the only clouds in the sky are fluffy cotton puffs, and you know this balmy weather won't last forever. You know you should spend time in New England's museums and cultural attractions, but you feel like walking through museum corridors as much as cleaning your bathroom. You should be outdoors getting exercise and enjoying the weather; guilt wins out over culture.

In winter, when darkness drops like a lead curtain at 4 P.M. and it is 10 above zero—that is when you can, with a clear conscience, be admiring early American interior design in an Historic Deerfield colonial house or delighting in the artistic handiwork of Norman Rockwell.

Admittedly, the cost of heating and the dearth of sightseers causes many northern New England attractions to close their doors until May. But then there is the exceptional Currier Gallery of Art in Manchester, New Hampshire, featured in this chapter; it is not necessary to travel to Boston, Hartford, or New Haven to see fine art.

In southern New England, you can see several of our major historical and general-interest sites. Most are in Massachusetts, the centrally-located New England state which is easily accessible via interstate highways. These are the places to visit when you are afflicted with cabin fever, and you know you won't be walking around in shirt-sleeves for what seems like light-years. Maybe even to evade the ski slopes.

HIGGINS ARMORY MUSEUM

A chance to meet your knight in shining armor and let your imagination take you to the times of chivalry and Camelot await you at the Higgins Armory Museum

ONCE UPON A TIME THERE LIVED A MAN—A GIANT TO MANY—WHO built a castle and filled it with knights in armor. Some of them were to stand guard constantly, others were to ride horseback, and still more were forever to be locked in combat.

Soon he had more armor and weapons than anybody else in his realm, and it was said you would have to journey hundreds of miles to see any grander collection.

But the closest this man ever got to seeing a live knight in action was in a movie theater, for he lived in the 20th century in a not so distant land called Worcester, Massachusetts.

True, he was a giant, but one of the industrial sort. His name was John Woodman Higgins, a central Massachusetts steel magnate whose interest in early armor led him on acquisition hunts to all parts of the globe.

The Higgins Armory opened in 1931, and although Higgins died in 1961, his assemblage still takes visitors on a trip back to the time of knights and chivalry. Visitors may admire the several dozen suits of armor, the many antiquated weapons, the original (and reproduction) stained glass, and the varied art works all displayed in a setting inspired by a Gothic castle.

As you start touring the museum, be prepared to have some of your Hollywood celluloid myths shattered.

You may recall seeing in big studio film productions depictions of battles in which a knight fell off his horse and could not pick himself up. Here you learn that knights did not become sitting ducks on the ground. Suits of armor were not prohibitively bulky, and a knight who fell from a horse in battle could right himself quickly.

You also hear that armor was not burdensome due to its excessive weight. It is true combat armor tipped the scales at 40 to 80 pounds, and armor used specifically for jousts usually weighed between 80 and 120 pounds. But the armor was distributed evenly from head to toe, and today's backpackers who carry 100 pounds of supplies certainly have things tougher.

As you walk through the halls, you become aware that all suits of armor did not look the same. Purpose and fashion were two main reasons for variety in style. A suit to be used for warfare was lighter and less cumbersome than one used in a jousting tournament, for example.

Trendiness was in flower, too. When you gaze at the Maximilian armor, you think that only Bigfoot could have comfortably worn this suit. But it reflects the civilian clothing style of Germany circa 1525.

There also is armor from France, Spain, England, and Japan, whose early Samurai helmets contained an opening at the top through which the warrior's pigtail poked. There is even a sample of the type used in colonial America.

Should you visit on a weekend, you and your children might volunteer to be amateur models. During these presentations, visitors in the audience are called up to the stage and asked to try on the latest fashions from the Tower of London.

One visitor was fitted with a padded doublet followed by a shirt of iron rings called "mail." This answered the much asked question, "What did a knight wear under his suit of armor?" You will be shown that because the iron rings were so tightly riveted and close together, the shirt was very hard to pierce.

A younger volunteer tried on a helmet, confirmed the fact that knights could see just fine, thank you, through the narrow slit for the eyes, and then allowed himself to be bopped on the head with a sword by a staff interpreter demonstrating armor's protective capabilities. In fact, armor didn't become obsolete until gunpowder was commonly used.

Mother Nature was the biggest threat to the knight's well-being. During the course of a battle in hot weather, heat exhaustion and heat stroke, often leading to heart attacks, were common.

Weapons of the knight's era, including swords, flails, maces and lances are a few of the many related items to be seen. Not all the armor is from the Renaissance period. Greek and Roman helmets can be examined but, surprisingly, very little armor from the medieval period exists in the museum (or anywhere else for that matter).

And not all armor was worn by humans. Dogs and horses were suited up as well, and canine-fitted armor is on display. One of the rarest items is Roman horse armor, found in 1922 in the armory tower of the city walls of a community destroyed in 256 A.D. But the most effective armor for animals is natural, and there is even an exhibit featuring an armadillo.

Where was a knight's suit of armor kept when not worn? The late 15th-century French oak armor chest provides the answer. Finer suits were wrapped in linen and kept in these chests until needed, which accounts for the well-preserved specimens today.

Renaissance stained glass is another eye-catcher. Come on a sunny day to see the glass sparkle.

In 1986 and 1987, the museum was renovated and expanded. One of the most innovative additions is the Quest Gallery on the second floor. It is a do-touch exhibit for both children and adults. You can try on a replica helmet or other article of medieval style clothing, make your own brass rubbing, play a game of chess, or take in a video on Life during the Renaissance.

Visitors standing in the midst of the museum's Great Hall can hear the clatter of dueling swords, as part of the museum's new sound and light show, recreating the experience of a medieval joust. It lasts about 10 minutes and is presented several times a day.

Location: The Higgins Armory Museum is at 100 Barber Avenue in Worcester. From Interstate 290, take exit 20 and follow Burncoat Street north to Randolph Road. Turn left onto Randolph Road and continue a

182 New England's Special Places

half mile to the museum. The armory is on the left. From Interstate 190, take exit 1 onto Route 12 north and follow across railroad tracks. Take a sharp right onto Barber Avenue and follow it less than a quarter mile to the museum at the intersection of Barber Avenue and Randolph Road. **Admission** is charged. **Hours:** Tuesday through Saturday, morning and afternoon; Sunday, afternoon only. Closed Monday except in July and August. **Allow** 45 minutes to an hour and a half. **Information:** Higgins Armory Museum, 100 Barber Avenue, Worcester, MA 01606; (508) 853-6015. **Note:** The live demonstrations (or in some cases, a film) are offered only on weekends most of the year, and it is recommended that you plan your visit when one is scheduled. In July and August, they are scheduled daily.

CHARLESTOWN NAVY YARD

Photo by Michael Schuman

A modern-day sailor, Seaman Apprentice Jerry Mullins, stands at the helm of
USS Constitution.

"THE MEN LIVED LIKE KENNELED DOGS," WROTE ONE SAILOR WHO
served a stint on the USS *Constitution* in the early 19th century.

When you see the limp hammocks on the *Constitution* and try reclining
in one at the nearby USS Constitution Museum, try to imagine rows of
these rocking with the waves in a cramped, stench-filled, claustrophobic
hold. Kenneled dogs couldn't have had it much worse.

After you board the oldest commissioned warship afloat in the world
and walk through the museum devoted to the *Constitution* and its era,
you realize that it took more than skills and guts to survive a tour of duty
in the U.S. Navy 150 years ago.

It didn't pay to be sick—or even confess sickness—on board the *Constitution*. As our guide, Seaman Apprentice Jerry Mullins from Dallas,
Texas, explained, the sick bay was in the ship's bow, the worst place to
be in rough seas. But that was the intent. Men admitted to sick bay lost
their daily rum ration, that moment of enjoyment that made life at sea

worth living. This threatened loss served as a hefty incentive to stay healthy.

But if an enlisted man died from illness or injury on board, there was no need to worry about funeral expenses. His body was wrapped in a hammock and tossed overboard.

Space was at a premium. One sea bag for storage of personal articles was shared by four men. The "head" was nothing more than four holes cut in a plank, mercifully placed at the head of the ship (hence the name) where the winds tend to blow towards the open sea. Cleanliness was not next to Godliness; it was common for men to bathe once every five or six months. "But I took one just a few weeks ago," joked Jerry Mullins with a deadpan expression Bob Newhart would envy.

A walk on the upper two decks shows you the sole purpose of the *Constitution*. The spar deck boasts cannonades that fired a 32-pound solid shot to a range of 400 yards. On the next level down is the gun deck. (The average height of adult men was four to six inches shorter than it is today; you have to duck to walk comfortably around the gun deck.) Each of the 30 long guns weighs three and a half tons; the shot from one could pierce 20 inches of wood at 1,000 yards.

None ever punctured the sides of the *Constitution*, thus earning it the nickname "Old Ironsides." Apprentice Seaman Mullins told us that in battle, shots bounced off the sides of the great ship. It was made of oak— not iron—and it had a record of being in 42 battles and never losing one.

All guides on board are sailors in the United States Navy and, like Jerry Mullins, serve as part of 18 months of volunteer honor duty. ("The only real difference between Dallas and Boston," smiled Texan Mullins, "is the accent. People are people wherever you go.")

If you are fortunate to visit on a dry day, you will see the guides wearing replicas of 19th-century Navy uniforms. Unfortunately, we last visited on a rainy Saturday afternoon when they were outfitted in more modern dress.

After touring the ship, it is worth your while to walk across the parking lot and spend some time inside the USS Constitution Museum. If you are used to stuffy "hands-off" museums, this one will be a welcome change. Hands-on exhibits beckon both young and old, maritime history buffs and quizzical landlubbers.

As well as climbing into flimsy hammocks, a 20th-century visitor can try raising reproductions of sails and steering a ship's wheel on a gently rocking deck. This is a museum where entertainment and education mesh fully.

For example, head to the computer terminals to test your skills as a navigator. You get to play sea captain as the computer terminal challenges you to safely sail the *Constitution,* as part of a fleet, from Charlestown to Gibraltar in no more than 22 days.

A sample problem? The computer will tell you on the sixth day at sea that salt water has seeped into your fresh water supply, ruining a substantial portion of it. The computer then gives you—the captain—a number of options: A. Use half normal daily rations, which would conserve water but lower morale; B. Continue with full rations, but probably run out of water unless a passing ship can help out within the next few days; C. Go back to Charlestown for more water, but lose valuable time. It's your choice; but remember you have to reach Gibraltar on time with a safe and healthy crew.

Sailors' knots, medical equipment, ship's documents, and scale models (on weekends and selected weekdays, you will see ship model-makers in action) make up some of the other exhibits here. You need not be a weekend sailor or military historian to enjoy the USS Constitution Museum, since few displays are very technical; the majority are designed to appeal to the layperson. How much did a U.S. Navy captain earn in 1812? From what are sails made? How did men tell time aboard the *Constitution* before clocks were on board? The answers await you at the museum.

Another vessel berthed at the Charlestown Navy Yard lets visitors explore life aboard a warship 130 years after the time of the *Constitution.* The USS *Cassin Young* is a World War II destroyer that served in the South Pacific in 1944 and 1945, and later saw action in the Korean conflict.

Though built in San Pedro, California, *Cassin Young* is representative of the 14 Fletcher Class destroyers built in the Charlestown Navy Yard during World War II. It is named for a Navy captain who was awarded the Congressional Medal of Honor for his service at Pearl Harbor on December 7, 1941. Less than a year later, Captain Young was killed while in command on the bridge of a heavy cruiser during the Battle of Guadalcanal.

The ship's first combat action occurred in April 1944, supporting air strikes on Japanese strongholds in the Caroline Islands. *Cassin Young* then played major roles in the capture of Saipan, Guam and Tinian and, in August 1944, joined aircraft carrier forces heading south for air attacks preceding the invasion of the Philippines. She also took part in the invasions of Iwo Jima and Okinawa in April 1945. But on July 29 of that year, 16 days before Japan surrendered, she was hit by a kamikaze-suicide plane. Although *Cassin Young* regained power within 20 minutes of the attack, the casualties were high: 22 men dead and 45 wounded. *Cassin Young* was later awarded the Navy Unit Commendation for her service and gallantry while in battle off Okinawa.

Cassin Young was decommissioned in 1946, brought back to duty in Korea, logged more than 50,000 miles in an around-the-world-cruise in 1954 and decommissioned again in 1960. She has been open to the public in Charlestown since June 1981.

Location: Take Interstate 93 (Southeast Expressway) to Route 1 north and exit at Constitution Road; follow the signs to the immediate parking area. **Admission** is free to USS *Constitution* and USS *Cassin Young*. **Admission** is charged to enter the USS Constitution Museum. **Hours:** Daily for USS *Constitution* and USS *Cassin Young;* daily except Thanksgiving, Christmas and New Year's Day for the USS Constitution Museum. **Allow** a half hour to tour USS *Constitution* and a half hour to tour USS *Cassin Young*. **Allow** 45 minutes to an hour to visit the USS Constitution Museum. **Information:** Boston National Historical Park, 15 State Street, Boston, MA 02109; (617) 242-5670 for USS *Constitution* and USS *Cassin Young*. USS Constitution Museum, P.O. Box 1812, Boston, MA 02129; (617) 426-1812. **Note:** Usually a guided tour is given on the *Constitution* but on busy days, visitors walk around the ship on their own and can ask questions of Navy personnel; in the off-season, there should be few days when it is too busy for guided tours. To get the full tour of USS *Cassin Young*, sign up in advance at the Navy Yard Visitor Center. The tours aboard both ships involve walking up and down narrow steep stairs, so wear good walking shoes. It can be chilly at the waterfront, so dress accordingly.

USS NAUTILUS

Could Jules Verne ever have imagined life under the sea in this namesake of his fictional Nautilus?

THE MISSION WAS SECRET, SO SECRET IN FACT THAT FOR WELL OVER half their journey, the crew of USS Nautilus did not even know where they were going.

From New London, Connecticut to Seattle, the men were kept in the dark, both literally and figuratively. But once USS Nautilus, the world's first nuclear-powered submarine, reached Seattle, crew members were given the chance to transfer upon hearing of the true mission of Nautilus's voyage: to be the first ship to pass under the geographic North Pole.

Said Nautilus Commander William R. Anderson of his crew some time later, "They did not resent the fact that we had to wait quite a while before cutting them in on the plans. Not that we didn't trust them, but we didn't want to put them in a position of making a possible slip."

Not a single crew member left the ship in Seattle. But dangerous ice conditions forced Nautilus to turn back. A second attempt also failed, but the third try was successful and on August 3, 1958 Nautilus sailed beneath the masses of ice at the North Pole. The ice appeared as a dense shadowy presence on a closed circuit television, or when it was thin enough for sufficient light to penetrate, on the periscope.

Walk through Nautilus today and you enter the world of the submarine crewman in 1958 when this vessel was making headlines for accomplishing feats that Jules Verne and other far-sighted dreamers only imagined.

While Nautilus once roamed all corners of the globe, its home today is in the waters of the U.S. Submarine Base in Groton, Connecticut. Adjacent is the Submarine Force Library and Museum, a hands-on voyage into the storied world of submarines.

The USS Nautilus was built here in Groton and christened in 1954 by then First Lady Mamie Eisenhower. It was only natural that local boosters felt the grand sub belonged here in her retirement. But other communities with a maritime heritage like San Diego; Bremerton, Washington; Charleston and Annapolis also had their eyes on her. It was a combination of strong grass roots support and intense lobbying that brought Nautilus back to the place she was born, and Nautilus and the museum opened to the public in April, 1986.

As you wander through corridors with the spare room of a Honda Civic you will realize that the submarine was no place for claustrophobics. Your fat Uncle Fred would have trouble fitting through; yet there is a Navy saying that goes. "There is room for everything aboard a submarine except a mistake."

Practical Yankee ingenuity was utilized in order to make enough room for 116 men in space 319 feet long and 28 feet wide. If you think you had it tough sharing a room in college or with a sibling at home, step up and look inside the bunk room which slept ten enlisted men. Rows of cots—three, then four, then three—are stacked one atop another and each man slept just two feet from the one next to him. A little white bag was kept at each cot for personal articles and the air was often fouled with odors of sweat, cigarettes and cooking.

Officers' bunks were larger than those of enlisted men but only the commanding officer had a room to himself. Prime use of space was made possible by building beds and sinks that folded when not in use; and you will see that the skimpy kitchen was no place for anyone to overindulge at mealtime.

After-dinner entertainment often consisted of a game of cards—two mannequins in the enlisted men's mess are hard at play—catching up on required or pleasure reading, or perhaps conversation on what the men missed most from home. About five snapshots of recognizable starlets and other comely models from the 1950s are scattered about the sub, indicating what the men missed most. (Parents, relax! For the sake of youngsters, the photos rate no worse than PG.)

Paperwork of a more vital nature is posted outside the ship's office where you will see Nautilus's position plotted on a chart: "3 August 1958; 4,844 nautical miles since Honolulu, 0 miles to the North Pole." A congratulatory telegram from President Eisenhower and an original copy of Jules Verne's classic *Twenty Thousand Leagues Under the Sea*, which also featured a submarine named Nautilus and was given as a gift to the crew, are on view.

In addition to the North Pole crossing, Nautilus accomplished other feats, once cruising over 3,000 miles from the Panama Canal to San Diego completely submerged. But one thing she thankfully never did was discharge one of her 20 torpedoes in battle.

To learn about subs employed in war and just about anything else you want to know about the rigors of submarine life, spend some time inside the Submarine Force Library and Museum, connected to Nautilus by a walkway.

Filmed highlights of submarine action during World War II complement a scale model, one-sixth the size of a World War II fleet sub; its engine, maneuvering room, forward and after torpedo rooms are all labeled. Although this sub was developed just 12 years before Nautilus, it could only be comfortably submerged for 12 hours.

Life on a wartime sub is dramatized by posted facts that jump out at you—only three toilets per 80 men, for example. But in order to keep morale up, men were allowed to gamble at cards, a pastime usually not condoned by the Navy. An unusual deck of playing cards custom-made for submarine men is displayed. Black outlines surround red hearts and diamonds, permitting men to see the suit of the cards they held while wearing night adaptation goggles.

Preferential treatment for submariners didn't stop at gambling. Their food was the best of any Navy grub. Displayed is a Christmas dinner menu, tempting the crew with roast tom turkey, baked ham, giblet gravy with bread dressing, and pumpkin pie and fruit cake for dessert.

Santa Claus may not have visited the ocean-bound men on that Christmas but he did appear to a submarine crew that journeyed to the North Pole four years after Nautilus's pioneering trip. An absurd-looking photo of the bearded fat man greeting Navy officers documents it. There is also a photo of the world's first polar baseball game; it's posted next to a sample of North Pole water.

The most popular stop among museum-goers is the cluster of three periscopes. Wait your turn, then focus your sights on your car in the parking lot, Nautilus in the water, or any unsuspecting person walking outdoors within range of the periscope's powers.

Over 100 years ago, Jules Verne wrote the following in *Twenty Thousand Leagues Under the Sea:* "On the Nautilus, men's hearts never fail them . . . this is the perfection of vessels."

The future seen by the prophetic Verne is on view in Groton today.

Location: USS Nautilus Memorial and the Submarine Force Library and Museum is at the U.S. Naval Submarine Base at the intersection of Military Highway and Crystal Lake Road. From Interstate 95, take exit 86 onto Route 12 heading north. Continue straight up Route 12 for a mile; at the intersection with Crystal Lake Road, turn left until you reach Nautilus and the museum. **Admission** is free. **Hours:** Year-round; Tuesday, afternoon only mid-April through mid-October; closed Tuesdays the rest of the year. **Allow** one and a half to two and a half hours to tour Nautilus and the museum. Much will depend on your level of interest. **Information:** Nautilus Memorial/Submarine Force Library and Museum, Box 571, Naval Submarine Base New London, Groton, CT 06349; (203) 449-3174 or 1-800-343-0079.

HISTORIC DEERFIELD

All that glitters is not silver. The Henry Needham Flynt Silver and Metalware Collection at Historic Deerfield also boasts the works of America's finest pewterers.

"THE STREET IS ONE MEASURED MILE, RUNNING NORTH & SOUTH ... There is a gate at each end of the Street, & about 60 houses in better style than any in the towns I saw."

> *Diary of Reverend William Bentley*
> *Deerfield, Massachusetts*
> *March, 1788*

"It is not excelled by anything I have ever seen, not excepting the Bay of Naples."

> *John Quincy Adams*

The Street is still called simply, The Street—with capital letters—in the western Massachusetts town that earned these accolades. You can still walk The Street in the section known as Historic Deerfield and see the handsome houses with their appealing yards. But today, you can also satisfy your curiosity by stepping inside a dozen of these once privately owned homes that date from the early 1700s to the mid-1800s.

Historic Deerfield differs from re-created villages like Mystic Seaport or Old Sturbridge. The majority of the homes are in their original locations. There is no turnstile at the entrance; you can walk up and down The Street as often as you wish for no charge. To enter the buildings, however, you pay an admission fee.

Historic Deerfield does not highlight colonial crafts, with tour guides in period dress. Nor are the roles of original residents play-acted. The emphasis here is on furnishings and architecture, rather than on life as it used to be. And unlike Sturbridge, Mystic, and the others, you won't want to spend the better part of a day walking in and out of the buildings lining The Street.

Executive Director Donald Friary tells of a woman from Scotland who, while visiting Historic Deerfield, made the fatal mistake of trying to cram too many houses in a one-day outing. "She came up to me afterwards and said, 'I have visual indigestion. I have seen too much.' "

"For the first time visitor," Friary recommends, "four hours is the optimum time here."

Take some time to see the free video presentation in the Hall Tavern Information Center, which presents an introduction to the homes and personalities of early Deerfield. Even on slow days it is shown continuously.

The homes frozen in time have distinct personalities, according to the guides. For example, the Ashley House was the home of Deerfield's Tory minister, Jonathan Ashley, and his writing desk will mean more to you after you hear about his controversial stand in the years prior to the American Revolution. Ashley believed in no separation of church and state and said that "you can only get to Heaven if you stand behind the King."

A few steps to the south of the Ashley House is the home of one of Deerfield's most colorful 19th-century residents, George Sheldon, the grey-bearded town historian. In addition to keeping track of Deerfield's past, he developed his own rules for longevity: 1. Eat a doughnut and coffee for breakfast. 2. Never worry about the weather. 3. Never open a window in any weather, winter or summer. And, said Sheldon, "you will live to a ripe old age."

We won't vouch for the therapeutic benefits of doughnuts and coffee but something must have clicked, for Sheldon died at the age of 98 in 1916.

Actually, said guide Pat Spofford as she showed us the Sheldon-Hawks House, it was common in Sheldon's day to believe that drafts from an open window could cause tuberculosis. When she showed us the nonagenarian's tidy sleeping quarters, we could see that he certainly was safe from the night air; there are no windows in his room.

Across from the Sheldon-Hawks House is a humble home currently being refurbished. Visitors to the disemboweled Ebenezer Hinsdale Williams House are given a 45-minute lesson in home restoration.

Friary and his wife Grace, the public relations director, both recommend that first-time sightseers make an effort to see the Wells-Thorn House. It is easily recognized by its startling sky blue exterior.

The house, built in 1717 and added to in 1754, has seven rooms, each furnished on the basis of household inventories that were compiled by Deerfield residents between 1725 and 1830. The rooms are toured chronologically, showing the evolution of decorative style in a rural New England village over a span of a little more than a century.

The visitor starts, for example, in a Spartan room from 1725, meagerly furnished with a primitive fireplace, a few tools, a sack of grain, and a small barrel, and proceeds through the early Victorian period. Even the Wells Thorn attic is outfitted in period, containing an accumulation of 105 years of residents' belongings, from plain and practical spinning wheels to elaborately gilded mirrors.

Location: Heading north on Interstate 91, take exit 24. Heading south, take exit 25. Then go six miles north on Routes 5 and 10 until you reach Historic Deerfield. **Admission** is charged to enter the houses. There is no charge to walk The Street. **Hours:** Daily except for Thanksgiving, Christmas Eve day, and Christmas. **Allow** a half hour to tour each house. **Information:** Historic Deerfield, Box 321, Deerfield, MA 01342; (413) 774-5581. **Note:** House tours are limited to six persons per guide; keep that in mind if you are visiting on a busy day. Tickets are good for two consecutive days.

OLD STURBRIDGE VILLAGE

Photo by Robert S. Arnold, courtesy Old Sturbridge Village

It appears like a Christmas card that has come to life: a sleigh ride through the streets of Old Sturbridge Village. And you can take one, too!

THE LANDSCAPE IS COVERED WITH A WINTERTIME DRESSING; STARK trees expose their brown branches in the brisk air and the spacious Green is snow-covered.

The pace is peaceful. There are even times when village interpreters outnumber tourists.

But life at Old Sturbridge Village in Sturbridge, Massachusetts, goes on, authentically reflecting early 19th-century activities day by day, season by season.

Just as we adjust to the changing seasons, this living history museum alters its representations of life 150 years ago according to the time of year. It is worth visiting in the winter and early spring, as well as when the colorful hills and valleys beckon in the fall.

A wisp of smoke curls out from a chimney, and you inhale the crisp scent of burning wood. Out by the Freeman Farmstead you see a team of oxen hauling logs. Inside the homes, toasty fires crackle, singing their own wintertime songs. And you feel as if you have Old Sturbridge Village all to yourself.

For early 19th-century Americans, winter was a quiet period, with necessary farm chores at a minimum, and the best time of the year for socializing. You see evidence of this no matter when in the winter you visit; but Old Sturbridge Village's off-season special events are especially lively.

Over Washington's Birthday weekend, the appetizing aroma of baking entices you into the houses to see villagers preparing Washington cakes prior to one of the biggest celebrations of the 1830s, the George Washington Birthday Ball.

Although Old Sturbridge Village may not actually schedule such a gala ball, Washington's Birthday interpreters prepare for it, cooking fancy foods, among them the Washington Cake.

Ingredients for this pound cake included: sugar, butter, two eggs, wine, milk, rosewater, nutmeg, raisins and white flour. The key item is the white flour, which unlike rye that many people grew on their own, had to be purchased and was rarely used.

Special services in the village meeting house honor the first president, delivered directly from an old text; but mercifully they have been cut down from a few hours to about 30 minutes.

More secular praise takes the form of a 19th-century toasting ceremony in the village tavern. Don't be shy when it comes to joining in with the crowd's roaring cries of, "Here! Here!" Keep in mind that many who were living in the 1830s served with Washington in New England in 1775 and 1776; to these veterans, the praise of their leader had personal significance.

If cooking is your craft, consider the often-scheduled Dinner In A Country Village, where you are encouraged to help prepare a hearth-cooked meal before dining on it by candlelight.

In the early evening you might help, baking rolls and apple pie in the beehive oven, heating vegetables in cast iron cooking pans, or preparing roast beef before setting it on the spit in the reflector oven by the fire. Kitchen phobics can lend a hand by splitting wood or kindling a fire in the hearth.

Mulled cider, cheese toast, and other snacks are offered as while-you-work-hors d'oeuvres. You will hear about 19th-century cooking methods while helping out in the kitchen; tales of early American life in New England and 19th-century table manners are offered during dinner. Morells (similar to tic-tac-toe played with corn and beans), Fox and Geese, backgammon, checkers, charades, and pick-up-sticks serve as after-dinner entertainment.

You can also enjoy these games at Old Sturbridge Village by Candlelight.

If you find any special events scheduled in December, you can assume they are in lieu of Christmas entertainment. New Englanders were among the last to observe Christmas as a public holiday. Because Old Sturbridge Village believes in keeping its events historically accurate, you will find food, music, and games, but no mention of Christmas in songs or in decorations.

Relax between games with sips of hot mulled cider and syllabub, or snacks of crackers, cheese, or meat platters. Period music is performed in the meeting house; magic tricks and puppet shows take place, too.

Want instruction in early crafts? Attend one of the Crafts-At-Close-Range workshops, scheduled often in the colder months. Learn the techniques of blacksmithing, tinsmithing, hearth cooking, or using a drawknife to craft a bucket for your own use. During these day-long sessions, you may also pick up the finer points of creating a basket by hand or imitating the best work of Sturbridge's own tinsmith.

While one session won't turn you into a master craftsman, you will leave with a better understanding of the techniques, time, and tools.

Location: From the Massachusetts Turnpike (Interstate 90), take exit 9 onto Route 20 and follow the signs. From Interstate 84, take exit 3 onto Route 20 and follow the signs. **Admission** is charged. **Hours:** Daily, year-round; closed Mondays in winter, Christmas, and New Year's Day. **Allow** at least four hours for a regular visit. Call or write for details or for the length of special events and functions. **Information:** Old Sturbridge Village, Old Sturbridge Village Road, Sturbridge, MA 01566; (508) 347-3362. **Note:** While the events listed in this article may not always be scheduled, they are included to suggest the kinds of winter activities and the atmosphere at Old Sturbridge Village. We strongly recommend you call first before driving any distance to attend any one specific event. Picnic tables are on the grounds for human polar bears or warm-weather visitors. There is a lot of walking here; wear comfortable shoes. The hearing-impaired can call the Telecommunications Device for the Deaf (TDD) number: (508) 347-5383.

THE NORMAN ROCKWELL MUSEUM AT THE OLD CORNER HOUSE

Photo by Louie Lamone, courtesy Norman Rockwell Museum at The Old Corner House

Norman Rockwell, pictured at work in his studio, made Stockbridge, Massachusetts' Main Street world famous. See his works and the scenery that inspired him in Stockbridge.

WE PEERED THROUGH THE FRONT WINDOW OF OLD MR. SHUFFLETON'S barber shop. In the back room, the old boys were playing happy tunes on the fiddle, the clarinet, and sundry other familiar tune-makers.

Mr. Shuffleton's furry tabby rested by the pot-bellied stove, looking in amusement at the guys making music. Fire gleamed in the stove, long after everyone had quit work. Even the push broom was at rest, sloping against a rear wall. We examined the broom closely and saw the evidence of its workday, newly clipped hairs it had swept stuck to the broom fibers.

We turned away from Shuffleton's window and admired another scene, an elderly sailor and a boy looking out to sea. We turned again and saw a young man leaving for college. Then there was a hungry family drooling at the sight of a Thanksgiving Day feast about to be served.

We were in the Norman Rockwell Museum at the Old Corner House in Stockbridge, Massachusetts, and the scenes were painted on canvas. This museum, the only permanent public display of Norman Rockwell's original paintings, is the repository for hundreds of his oils. About 50 are exhibited at one time, and are described on a guided tour.

Here you can appreciate the details in Rockwell's art that aren't discernable on the prints, mugs, ash trays, and other reproductions of his paintings. Let's go back to *Shuffleton's Barber Shop* and take a closer look.

If you see a print of this, you can appreciate the tone of what Rockwell is depicting; it's a happy scene in a country barber shop. Others might be cute or funny or solemn. But as prints, they are all flat. The color isn't as vivid as in the oil. The illusion of depth isn't as realistic. The details are lost.

Seeing a Rockwell work of art in person is like seeing for the first time a famous man-made landmark or location of an historic event. You might recall photographs of Big Ben or the White House, but they pale when compared to the real thing.

In *Shuffleton's Barber Shop*, which originally appeared—like so many of Rockwell's creations—on the cover of the *Saturday Evening Post* (April 29, 1950), you can easily pick out the boots drying in front of the stove, the comic books on the shelf in the left foreground, and the dingy walls.

Then notice the fine detail: the clipped hairs on the push broom; the crack in the pane of glass that is the shop's front window; it establishes depth. Look closer at it and you will see a hint of blue along its edge, a bit of discoloration that can't be detected in the print.

Such details are also brought to our attention in *Freedom From Want*, the Thanksgiving Day table scene, part of Rockwell's famous Four Freedoms series based on a speech given by President Franklin Roosevelt. Rockwell had to work with numerous shades of white: both the tablecloth and the china are white; but the china shows up distinctly, as does the linen. The drinking glasses are clear, as is the water inside them, but we see both distinctly.

You might not associate Norman Rockwell with Alfred Hitchcock, but the artist and the filmmaker both shared a common trait. Each found it irresistible to place themselves in their creations. In the bottom right corner of *Freedom From Want,* you see the artist sitting at the table, his head turned, looking back slyly towards his audience.

Rockwell's sense of humor is also apparent. Explaining that he always painted from live scenes and models, our guide told us that Rockwell said of the rotund Thanksgiving turkey, "That was the only time I ever ate a model."

A native of New York City, Rockwell moved to Arlington, Vermont in 1939 and then relocated in 1953 to Stockbridge, Massachusetts, where he lived until his death 25 years later. In both Arlington and Stockbridge, several of his models became local celebrities. While studying the 1950 painting *Marriage License,* with its nervous young couple and bored clerk anxious to quit for the day, we hear that the couple portrayed in the scene is still married, has four children and several grandchildren and live nearby.

Exhibited next to the finished *Marriage License* is a preliminary sketch. In a departure from most art galleries, this museum lets you see a few of the artist's ideas he rejected for various reasons.

The galleries at the Old Corner House are organized chronologically, and you see Rockwell's maturation as a painter and his concessions to modern times. Some paintings, notably the Four Freedoms series and the cheery *Stockbridge at Christmas,* are on permanent display. Others are rotated yearly, 30 percent to 40 percent replaced at one time.

Many ask whether Rockwell ever lived in the Old Corner House. The surprising and disappointing answer is no.

Because of the lack of exhibit space and the crowds that form—especially in the summer and on fall weekends—the collection will move to a new location two miles west of town but not until 1992 at the earliest.

Location: The Norman Rockwell Museum at the Old Corner House is on Main Street in Stockbridge. Take exit 2 off the Massachusetts Turnpike (Interstate 90) onto Route 102 and follow it into the village. **Admission** is charged. **Hours:** Daily; closed last two weeks in January, Thanksgiving, Christmas and New Year's Day. **Allow** 35 minutes for the tour. **Information:** The Norman Rockwell Museum at the Old Corner House, Stockbridge, MA 01262; (413) 298-3822. **Note:** Expect the museum to be busy in the summer and jammed on fall weekends; on such weekends, the crowds may be so big that the staff will have to dispense with guided tours and let visitors walk through on their own and ask questions. The gift shop is a utopia for Rockwell buffs with books, prints, calendars, china and other items sporting Rockwell's art.

In Vermont, there are two more museums devoted to Rockwell's art, though each showcases framed magazine covers or prints rather than original oils. The Norman Rockwell Museum in Rutland emphasizes Rockwell's art as it records American social history during his career; (802) 773-6095. At the Norman Rockwell Exhibition at the Arlington Gallery, Rockwell's former models are tour guides who tell the stories behind the paintings; (802) 375-6423.

OFF-SEASON IN ACADIA NATIONAL PARK

Courtesy: Bar Harbor Times

Appreciate the Atlantic's raging fury at Acadia National Park's Thunder Hole.

IF YOU WISH TO HEAD INTO THE WILDS ALONG THE MAINE COAST WITH-
out following a mile of cars or a sea of backpacks, head to Acadia National
Park during the off-season.

Acadia is one of the few spots along the eastern seaboard where the
mountains really do meet the sea. In the United States, for much of the
year, the rising sun first strikes the park's Cadillac Mountain. Though
only 1,530 feet above sea level, it is as pronounced as Jimmy Durante's
nose on a coastline otherwise known for sand and sea oats. Massive Otter
Cliffs, 110 feet in height and composed of granite, mark the highest
headlands on the Atlantic Coast north of Brazil.

There are many sights to be seen from the overlooks that dot the Park
Loop Road: for instance, the prominent precipice known as Schooner
Head, usually seen with waves breaking at its feet, and the placid Por-
cupine Islands rising above Frenchman's Bay like the rounded backs of
migrating whales.

Through the summer and much of the fall, however, the view is full of
cars and people. The awe-inspiring sights of Acadia are well known and
make it the second most visited national park in the country, after Great
Smoky Mountains National Park. Over 4,000,000 visitors enter Acadia
annually, most from May through October. For comparison purposes, the
year-round population of Maine is 1,182,000.

To see the scenery in solitude, come in the off-season. Whether you
plan to explore the park from inside a car or on a snowmobile, or with
cross-country skis, or snowshoes, you will be privy to the sound of roaring
waves, unsullied by the noise of traffic.

In fact, traditional summer vacationers would be well advised to make
an off-season pilgrimage, to explore this national park in quietude and see
it in its winter clothes—snowscapes along the ocean, crackling ice clinging
to low-lying shrubs, and wildlife unhidden by forests of thick foliage.

A park ranger says, "After a winter storm, the park is quite beautiful,
with snow all the way down to the ocean and build-ups of ice along the
rocks and granite ledges."

Though some of Park Loop Road is closed by snow much of the winter,
there are alternate routes for motorists. Many of the byways around
Mount Desert Island, on which most of Acadia sits, are town and state
roads and are always plowed, as are portions of Park Loop Road. The
winter visitor can even drive to the chasm known as Thunder Hole and
appreciate the Atlantic's raging fury. When waves crash into this hollow
in the rocks, the air at the rear is compressed and the result is a tumul-
tuous boom. The resonance is at its loudest following a storm, but avoid
this place during one.

To fully appreciate the serenity of Acadia in winter, leave the car behind and strap on a pair of skis. Glide through the woods, with the wind on your cheeks, pause and savor the world of the cross-country skier, listen to the sounds of winter by the ocean: waves breaking on the shore, the trickle of snow melting off of an evergreen branch in the sun, a deer dashing through the woods.

A total of forty-one miles of unplowed park roads are open to skiers, snowshoers and snowmobilers. (Acadia is one of the few national parks open for snowmobiling.)

Many winter visitors prefer to traverse the carriage paths. John D. Rockefeller, Jr., a one time Bar Harbor resident, built this network of paths when the century was young, stipulating that motorized access be limited. When free of snow cover, they are used by hikers, joggers, bicyclers, horseback riders, and, as in early times, folks in carriages. When enveloped with snow however, cross-country skiers and snow-shoers use the paths which are marked by gates, gate houses and stone bridges.

While there are no imposingly steep grades along the carriage paths, a staff member suggests that beginners would be happiest on the Eagle Lake and Witch Hole Pond loops in the northern part of the park, and on many of the loops emanating from Jordan Pond at the park's southern end. Accessibility to Jordan Pond is from Route 3 in Seal Harbor south of the park.

Eagle Lake loop is six miles long and begins just past Route 233 at the northwest corner of the lake, and is usually traversed in a clockwise direction. However, beginners might want to tackle it counter-clockwise in order to avoid a hefty climb at the lake's southern end. Witch Hole Pond Loop is just 3.3 miles long, but combined with the tiny Paradise Hill loop, it equals 4.6 miles total, and presents a stellar view of Hull's Cove and Frenchman's Bay.

Park rangers recommend that intermediate cross-country skiers head for the Giant Slide Loop, or the Around Mountain Loop (11.1 miles), which skirts Penobscot, Sargent and Parkman mountains. Both loops boast sufficient climbing to tire out most beginners but reward strong-legged skiers with peak scenery, as well as a sight of the small, plunging stream at Chasm Brook Bridge. The Around Mountain Loop is the longest of the carriage paths. Skiers may enter either loop from the Parkman Mountain parking lot.

If you are an advanced beginner or a fledgling intermediate, the path for you is Aunt Betty's Pond Loop, west of Eagle Lake. The sharp drop over six small bridges and the final climb may intimidate pure novices but the vistas of Cadillac Mountain and Eagle Lake are well worth it. Confident skiers might want to challenge the auto road ascending Cadillac Mountain.

Snowshoers have more alternatives than cross-country skiers. The loop road, carriage paths and the many miles of hiking trails are at their command. Snowmobilers are even granted access to two miles of the carriage paths.

Some advice for winter fun enthusiasts. Because of the park's coastal location, winter conditions are variable. Icy snows and freezing rains are common and a foot of snow in Bangor doesn't necessarily mean skiing at Acadia. Prospective snowshoers should be aware that the snow is often too shallow to cover roots and rocks. A call to the park in advance for up-to-date weather conditions is a good idea.

What about early spring and late fall? Come for the tranquility but be prepared for chilly temperatures. The majestic sights are yours and bare trees afford unobstructed views of the ocean, islands and wildlife, like deer, fox and coyotes. Bird watchers head to Acadia in fall and spring to see migrating flocks.

Of course, you can come to Acadia in any season for a vision of Mother Nature's grandest work on the Atlantic Coast, but to experience the park at its quietest, come in the off-season.

Location: Acadia National Park is along the northeastern coast of Maine, 164 miles north of Portland. From Route 1 in Ellsworth, take Route 3 south to the park. The Park Loop Road begins just south of Hulls Cove. **Admission** is free in winter. **Hours:** Daily, year-round. **Allow** four to six hours for a leisurely tour of the park, much longer for skiing or any other recreational activity. **Information:** Acadia National Park, P.O. Box 177, Bar Harbor, ME 04609; (207) 288-3338.

Note: In season, stop first at the visitor center at the start of the Park Loop Road. If the visitor center is closed, stop first at park headquarters on Route 233, three miles west of Bar Harbor. The park winter activities guide, which includes a detailed map highlighting plowed roads, carriage paths for skiers and snowshoers, and snowmobile routes, is a must for any off-season visitor. One of the park's two campgrounds, Blackwoods Campground, near Seal Harbor, is open all year and camping is free in winter. (To camp at Blackwoods in mid-summer, reservations through Mistix are necessary; the other campground, Seawall Campground, is open on a first come, first served basis in summer but is closed in winter.)

In winter, much of Bar Harbor closes up like a ghost town in Nevada. However, Cadillac Mountain Sports, 23 Cottage Street in Bar Harbor, rents cross-country skis and equipment; (207) 288-4532. Other stores renting equipment are in Ellsworth, about 10 miles north. For further information, contact the Bar Harbor Chamber of Commerce at (207) 288-3393.

THE CURRIER GALLERY OF ART

Courtesy: Currier Gallery of Art

The European countryside or the vast American West? No, it's our own New England: Moat Mountain, Intervale, New Hampshire *by Albert Bierstadt, part of the Currier Gallery of Art collections.*

WHERE IN NORTHERN NEW ENGLAND CAN YOU SEE THE WORKS OF such artists as Picasso, Remington, Copley and Calder? Or colonial American furniture, Tiffany glass, and Paul Revere silverworks?

All are under one roof in one of New England's most underpublicized art museums, The Currier Gallery of Art in Manchester, New Hampshire, once described as a "little gallery on a grand scale."

It takes just a few hours to wander through the Renaissance-style structure that was built to resemble a modest Italian palace; but within that time you will be exposed to works of art that would stand out in some of the nation's finest art museums.

And if you have been here previouisly but not within the past several years, you should plan a visit to see the new wings added in 1982. You will be pleased to see that the classical lines of the original Currier have been reinforced by the recent additions.

The museum itself dates back to 1929 and sits on the site of the home of bank president, attorney and former governor Moody Currier. This man of many hats stipulated in his will that following the death of his wife, Hannah, his property was to become a gallery of art for all the citizens of New Hampshire.

There was one major problem. Neither Moody nor Hannah were art collectors, and when the museum first opened the entire collection consisted of a handful of oils and watercolors, bequeathed by Manchester industrialist George A. Leighton.

Since then, the gallery has slowly but deliberately acquired significant works, among them: *John Greene,* a portrait by John Singleton Copley, was purchased in 1935; *Portrait of a Lady* by Lorenzo Costa (1947); *The Seine at Bougival* by Claude Monet (1949); *Dedham Mill* by John Constable (1950); *Spindrift* by Andrew Wyeth (1951); *Seated Nude* by Henri Matisse (1964); and *The Wounded Clown* by Georges Rouault (1964).

Picking one's personal favorite is up to you. There is Picasso's cubist *Woman Seated in a Chair,* which, with Monet's impressionist *Seine at Bougival,* would rank as two of any museum's top possessions.

You will see a gallery devoted to some of the museum's oldest masterpieces, mainly religious interpretations: *Madonna and Child With Angels,* an Italian tempera, dated back to about 1275; Pietro Perugino's tempera, *Madonna and Child* (circa 1495); Astorga Master's *Crucifixion* (circa 1520); and Joos Van Cleve's *Holy Family* (circa 1520–1525).

These latter two are good examples of the emergence of nature as a subject, previously seen only in the background of religious paintings. Landscapes didn't really become popular until 17th-century Dutch merchants bought pictures of their homes; a century later, English artists began to take seriously the art of landscape painting.

Gracing an entire wall is a captivating Franco-Flemish tapestry, *The Visit of the Gypsies* (circa 1490). You will have to study it to find all the different goings-on. It is easy to note the arrival of the king and queen of the gypsies, and you won't have to look hard to find the lord and lady who meet them. But search closely to scout out the gypsy child stealing the lady's purse.

The north country setting of Albert Bierstadt's *Moat Mountain, Intervale, New Hampshire* (painted about 1862) still exists as this great painter of American natural beauty saw it; but today it is hidden behind a modern development.

The beauty of New England is further represented in the watercolors by Childe Hassam (*Newfields, New Hampshire,* 1906), Winslow Homer

(*The North Woods*, 1894), and Edward Hopper (*House on Middle Street, Gloucester*, 1924).

Hopper's oil, *The Bootleggers* (1925), is a most intriguing work portraying a wave-tossed boat arriving at an ominous Victorian mansion. Georgia O'Keeffe's *Cross by the Sea* (1931) is fascinating in its simplicity.

Those who prefer colonial portraits will want to see the works of John Singleton Copley, John Trumbull, and Gilbert Stuart, while anybody who recalls the way Manchester looked over a generation ago should inspect *Amoskeag Canal* by Charles Sheeler. It was finished in 1948, a tribute to the former industrial greatness of this city on the Merrimack River.

To paintings and sculpture (Saint Gaudens, Rodin, Matisse and Remington are represented in the latter category), the Currier has added noteworty collections of decorative arts, including American furniture, glass, pewter, textiles, and silver. Don't miss the Levi Hutchins shelf clocks, the New Hampshire-made colonial chest-on-chest, the cotton-on-cotton coverlet, or the colossal weathervane that once topped the Amoskeag Mills in Manchester.

Location: The Currier Gallery of Art is at 192 Orange Street, Manchester. Heading north on Interstate 293, take exit 6 (Amoskeag Bridge exit). Bear to the right around the Holiday Inn and cross the bridge. Continue straight past Elm Street to Salmon Street. Continue straight on Salmon for seven blocks and turn right onto Beech Street; continue on Beech for seven blocks to Orange Street. The museum is at the corner of Beech and Orange Streets. Parking is on the street. **Admission** is free. **Hours:** Tuesday through Saturday, mornings and afternoons; Thursday evenings; Sunday afternoons. **Allow** one to three hours, depending greatly on your interest and "burn-out" levels. **Information:** The Currier Gallery of Art, 192 Orange Street, Manchester, NH 03104; (603) 669-6144. **Note:** Works from the museum's collection are rotated; not all are on view at one time. If you have your heart set on seeing one specific work, you may want to call or write ahead. In addition, a return visit might acquaint you with works you hadn't seen before. Concerts and films are presented regularly, and you can receive a schedule by writing to the Currier. Also, the Zimmerman House, which Frank Lloyd Wright designed for a Manchester doctor and his wife in 1950, was opened to the public by the Currier in 1990. It is a classic Wright Usonian house and certainly unique. Tours of the house leave from the Currier. Call for information.

ADDITIONAL LISTINGS

OTHER ATTRACTIONS DESCRIBED IN THIS BOOK ARE IN FULL OPERATION throughout the year:

Pilgrim Hall Museum, Plymouth, Massachusetts.
Webb-Deane-Stevens Museum, Wethersfield, Connecticut.
Bunker Hill Monument of Boston National Historical Park, Charlestown, Massachusetts.
"Whites of Their Eyes" at Bunker Hill Pavilion, Charlestown, Massachusetts.
John F. Kennedy National Historic Site, Brookline, Massachusetts.
John F. Kennedy Library and Museum, Dorchester, Massachusetts.
Museum of American Political Life, West Hartford, Connecticut.
Lowell National Historical Park, Lowell, Massachusetts.
Maine Maritime Museum, Bath, Maine.
Norlands Living History Center, Livermore, Maine.
Owls Head Transportation Museum, Owls Head, Maine.
Western Gateway Heritage State Park, North Adams, Massachusetts.
Hammond Castle, Gloucester, Massachusetts.
Naismith Memorial Basketball Hall of Fame, Springfield, Massachusetts.
International Tennis Hall of Fame, Newport, Rhode Island.
New England Sports Museum, Boston, Massachusetts.
The Computer Museum, Boston, Massachusetts.
Barnum Museum, Bridgeport, Connecticut.
New England Carousel Museum, Bristol, Connecticut.

In addition, these New England attractions not listed elsewhere in the book are among those open all year long.

Greenwich, CT. Audubon Center. (203) 869-5272.

Norwalk, CT. The Maritime Center. (203) 852-0700.

Norwich, CT. Slater Memorial Museum and Converse Art Gallery, (203) 887-2506.

Stamford, CT. Stamford Museum and Nature Center. (203) 322-1646.

West Hartford, CT. Science Museum of Connecticut. (203) 236-2961.

Windsor Locks, CT. New England Air Museum. (203) 623-3305.

Brunswick, ME. Bowdoin College Museum of Art. (207) 725-3275.

Brunswick, ME. Peary-MacMillan Arctic Museum. (207) 725-3416.

Portland, ME. Portland Museum of Art. (207) 775-6148.

Concord, MA. Concord Museum. (508) 369-9609.

Gloucester, MA. Cape Ann Historical Association. (508) 283-0455.

Lexington, MA. Museum of Our National Heritage. (617) 861-6559.

Salem, MA. Essex Institute. (508) 744-3390.

Salem, MA. Peabody Museum. (508) 745-9500.

Salem, MA. House of Seven Gables. (508) 744-0991.

Williamstown, MA. Sterling and Francine Clark Art Institute. (413) 458-9545.

Merrimack, NH. Anheuser-Busch, Inc. Brewery Tour and Clydesdale Hamlet. (603) 595-1202.

St. Johnsbury, VT. Fairbanks Museum and Planetarium. (802) 748-2372.

St. Johnsbury, VT. St. Johnsbury Athenaeum. (802) 748-8291.

Most museums and cultural centers and many historic sites in the following New England cities are also open throughout the year: Bridgeport, Mystic, Hartford, and New Haven, Connecticut; Boston, Cambridge, Worcester, and Springfield, Massachusetts; Providence, Rhode Island; and Burlington, Vermont.

Index

Abigail Adams House, 72
Acadia National Park, 201–204
Adams, Abigail Smith, 72
Adams, John, 45–48
Adams, John Quincy, 45–48
Adams National Historic Site, 46–48
Air Museum, New England, 209
Aldrich, Thomas Bailey, 32–33
Alstead, NH, 87
American Maple Products Corporation, 113
The American Museum of Fly-Fishing, 176
American Precision Museum, 113
Anheuser-Busch, Inc. Brewery Tour and Clydesdale Hamlet, 209
Aquidneck Island, RI, 24–27
Arlington, VT, 200
Arthur, Chester A., 56–60
Astor family, 124–127
Astor's Beechwood, 124–127
Audubon Center (Greenwich, CT), 208

Babcock-Smith House, 176
Bacon's Sugar House, 87
Bar Harbor, ME, 201–204
Barnum Museum, 167–170, 208
Barre, VT, 105–107
Barrett's Sugar House, 85, 87
Bascom's Sugar House, 87
Basketball Hall of Fame, 145–148, 208
Bath, ME, 97–100, 208
Battleship Cove and Marine Museum, 112
Beauport, 142
Belcourt Castle, 142
Bennington, VT, 42

Bennington Battle Monument, 42
Bennington Museum, 42
Billings Farm and Museum, 101–104
Birthplace
    Adams, John and John Quincy, 47–48
    Arthur, Chester A., 57, 58–60
    Coolidge, Calvin, 56
Blithewold Gardens and Arboretum, 142
Boothbay, ME, 171–173, 174
Boothbay Railway Village, 171–173, 174
Boston, MA, 38–41, 65–67, 155–158, 163–166, 183–186, 208
Boston National Historical Park, 41, 208
Bowdoin College Museum of Art, 209
The Breakers, 142
Bridgeport, CT, 167–170, 208
Bristol, CT, 208
Bristol, RI, 142
Brookline, MA, 208
Brown, John, House, 142
Bruce Museum, 208
Brunswick, ME, 209
Bunker Hill Momument, 38–41, 208
Bunker Hill Pavilion, 40, 41
Bush, George, 73
Butler-McCook Homestead, 176
Buttolph-Williams House, 21, 22

Calvin Coolidge Memorial Room in Forbes Library, 72
Campobello Island, New Brunswick, 61–64
Canterbury, NH, 89–92
Canterbury Shaker Village, 89–92

Cape Ann Historical Association, 209
Castle in the Clouds, 132–134
Castles, 115–142
Charlestown, MA, 41, 183–186, 208
Charlestown, NH, 28–30, 88
Charlestown Navy Yard, 41, 183–186
Chateau-Sur-Mer, 142
Churches, First Church of Christ (Old Wethersfield), 21, 22
Clarks' Sugar House, 87
Cleveland, Grover, 72
Colonial period sights, 9–42
The Computer Museum, 163–166, 208
Comstock, Ferre & Company, 21–22
Concord, MA, 42, 209
Concord, NH, 50, 51–52
Concord Museum, 209
Coolidge, Calvin, 56–60, 72, 73
Coolidge Homestead, 56, 59–60
Coventry, CT, 42
Cranberry World, 14, 15
Currier Gallery of Art, 205–207

Deerfield, MA, 191–193
The Depot Stock Exchange Antiques (Old Wethersfield), 22
Dinsmore Blacksmith Shop, 33
Dorchester, MA, 65–67, 208

East Granby, CT, 34–37
East Haddam, CT, 117–120
The Elms, 142
Enchanted Heart (Old Wethersfield), 22
Essex Institute, 209

Fairbanks Museum and
  Planetarium, 209
Fall River, MA, 95–96, 112
Faneuil Hall, 41
First Church of Christ (Old
  Wethersfield), 21, 22
The First House, 14–15
Forbes Library, 72
Fort Griswold State Park,
  42
Fort at No. 4, NH, 28–30
Franconia, NH, 152–154
Franklin Pierce Home-
  stead, 49–52
Fyler House, 42

Gardner, MA, 96
Gardner Heritage State
  Park, 96
Garfield, James A., 72
Gillette Castle, 117–120
Gillette, William, 118–119
Gloucester, MA, 121–123,
  142, 208, 209
Granite Quarry, Rock of
  Ages, 105–107
Green Animals, 176
Greenville, ME, 112
Greenwich, CT, 208
Groton, CT, 42, 188–190

Hale, Nathan, Homestead,
  42
Hammersmith Farm, 72
Hammond Castle, 121–123,
  208
Hammond, John Hays,
  121–123
Hampton, NH, 176
Hancock Shaker Village,
  112
Harlow's Sugar House, 87
Hartford, CT, 42, 176
Heritage State Park at
  Battleship Cove, 95–96
Heritage State Parks,
  Massachusetts, 93–96
Higgins Armory Museum,
  179–182
Hildene, 53–55
Hillsboro, NH, 49–52
Historic Deerfield, 191–193
Historic houses
  Abigail Adams, 72
  Adams', 45–48
  Arthur, Chester A.,
    birthplace, 57, 58–60

Babcock-Smith, 176
Butler-McCook Home-
  stead, 176
Buttolph-Williams, 21, 22
Coolidge Homestead, 56
Deerfield, 191–193
The First House, 14–15
Franklin Pierce Home-
  stead, 49–52
Fyler, 42
Hammersmith Farm, 72
Hildene, 53–55
House of Seven Gables,
  42, 209
Howland, 14
Hunter, 25–26, 27
John F. Kennedy Na-
  tional Historic Site,
  65, 67, 208
Lexington Historical So-
  ciety, 42
Mission, 42
Nathan Hale Homestead,
  42
Paul Revere's, 41
Portsmouth Trail, 42
Richard Sparrow, 14, 15
Roosevelt Home, 61–64
  16–27
House, 14–15
Thomas Bailey Aldrich,
  32
Wanton-Lyman-Hazard,
  26, 27
Wheelwright, 33
Woodstock Historical So-
  ciety's Dana House,
  176
Historic sites. *See also*
  Historic homes; Mili-
  tary history; Museums
Lowell National Histori-
  cal Park, 80–82, 84,
  208
Massachusetts Heritage
  State Parks, 93–96
Saugus Iron Works, 77–
  79
Slater Mill, 82–84
Western Gateway Heri-
  tage State Park, 93
Holyoke, MA, 96, 142, 176
Holyoke Heritage State
  Park, 96
Hooper Mansion, 142
House of Images (Old
  Wethersfield), 22

House of Seven Gables, 42,
  209
Howland House, 14, 15
Hunter House, 25–26, 27

Industries, 75–113
Infinity's Curiosity Shop
  (Old Wethersfield), 22
International Tennis Hall
  of Fame, 149151, 208

Jaffrey Center, NH, 87
Jeremiah Lee Mansion, 142
Jewelry by Neil Walsh
  (Old Wethersfield), 22
John Brown House, 142
John F. Kennedy Library
  and Museum, 65–67,
  208
John F. Kennedy National
  Historic Site, 65, 67,
  208

Keene, NH, 85, 87
Kennebunkport, ME, 173–
  175
Kennedy, John F., 65–67,
  72, 73
King Hooper Mansion, 142
Kingscote, 142

Lake Winnipesaukee, NH,
  132–134
Lawrence, MA, 95
Lawrence Heritage State
  Park, 95
Lee Mansion, 142
Lexington, MA, 42, 209
Lexington Historical Soci-
  ety houses, 42
Lincoln, Robert Todd, 53–
  55
Livermore Falls, ME, 108–
  111, 208
Living History Center,
  Norlands, 108–111,
  208
Lockwood, LeGrand, 138–
  139
Lockwood-Mathews Man-
  sion, 138–141
Lowell, MA, 80–82, 84, 95,
  208
Lowell Heritage State
  Park, 95
Lowell National Historical
  Park, 80–82, 84, 208

Lumberman's Museum, 112
Lynn, MA, 95
Lynn Heritage State Park, 95

Maine Maritime Museum, 97–100, 208
Maine transportation museums, 171–175
Manchester, NH, 205–207
Manchester, VT, 53–55, 176
Mansions, 115–142. *See also* Historic houses
Maple Grove Museum, 113
Maple sugar houses, 85–88
Marble House, 142
Marblehead, MA, 142
Marine museums
  Battleship Cove and, 112
  Maine Maritime, 97–100, 208
  Moosehead, 112
  Penobscott Marine, 112
The Maritime Center, 208
Maritime Museum, Maine, 97–100, 208
Massachusetts Urban Heritage State Parks, 93–96
Massacoh Plantation, 42
Mathews, Charles D., 139
Mayflower II, 12–13, 14–15
Merrimack, NH, 209
Merimack Valley Textile Museum, 112
Military history
  Bennington Battle Monument, 42
  Bunker Hill, 38–41
  Bunker Hill Monument, 208
  Charlestown Navy Yard, 183–186
  Fort at No. 4, NH, 28–30
  Fort Griswold State Park, 42
  Minuteman National Historical Park, 42
Milton, NH, 112
Minuteman National Historical Park, 42
Mission House, 42
Monuments
  Bennington Battle, 42
  Bunker Hill, 38–41, 208

Moosehead Marine Museum, 112
The Mulberry Tree (Old Wethersfield), 22
Museum of American Political Life, 68–71, 208
Museum of Our National Heritage, 209
Museums
  American Maple Products Corporation, 113
  of American Political Life, 68–71, 208
  American Precision, 113
  of Art
    Bowdoin College Museum 209
    Portland, 209
  Barnum, 167–170, 208
  Battleship Cove and Marine, 112
  Bennington, 42
  Billings Farm and, 101–104
  Boothbay Railway Village, 171–173, 174
  Bruce, 208
  Canterbury Shaker Village, 89–92
  The Computer, 163–166, 208
  Concord, 209
  Currier Gallery of Art, 205–207
  Fairbanks, and Planetarium, 209
  of Fly-Fishing, The American, 176
  Green Animals, 176
  Hancock Shaker Village, 112
  Higgins Armory, 179–182
  International Tennis Hall of Fame, 149–151, 208
  John F. Kennedy Library and, 65–67, 208
  Lumberman's, 112
  Maine Maritime, 97–100, 208
  Maple Grove, 113
  Massacoh Plantation, 42
  Merimack Valley Textile, 112
  Moosehead Marine, 112
  Musical Wonder House Music, 176

Mystic Seaport, 112
Naismith Memorial Basketball Hall of Fame, 145–148, 208
Nantucket Whaling, 112
Nautilus Memorial Submarine Force Library and, 187–190
New Bedford Whaling, 112
New England Air, 209
New England Carousel, 167–170, 208
New England Maple, 85, 86, 88
New England Ski, 152–154
New England Sports, 155–158, 208
New Hampshire Farm, 112
Norlands Living History Center, 108–111
The Norman Rockwell, at the Old Corner House, 197–199
Norman Rockwell, in Rutland, 200
Norman Rockwell Exhibition, 200
Old New-Gate Prison and Copper Mine, 34–37
Old Sturbridge Village, 194–196
Old York Historical Society, 16–19
of Our National Heritage, 209
Owls Head Transportation, 173, 174
Peabody, 209
Peary-MacMillan Arctic, 209
Penobscot Marine, 112
Pilgrim Hall, 13, 15, 208
Plimoth Plantation, 11–12
Richard Sparrow House, 14
Saugus Iron Works National Historic Site, 77–79
Science, of Connecticut, 209
Seashore Tolley, 173–175
Shaker, 112

Museums (*cont.*)
  Shelburne, 159–162
  Slater Memorial, and
    Converse Art Gallery,
    208
  Smith's Castle, 42
  Stamford, and Nature
    Center, 209
  Sterling and Francine
    Clark Art Institute,
    209
  Tuck Memorial, 176
  Vermont Marble Ex-
    hibit, 113
  Volleyball Hall of Fame,
    176
  Webb-Deane-Stevens
    Museum, 21, 22, 208
  Wells Auto, 175
  Wenham Historical As-
    sociation, 176
  Wilson, 42
  Yesteryears Doll and
    Miniature, 176
Musical Wonder House
  Music Museum, 176
Mystic, CT, 112
Mystic Seaport Museum,
  112

Naismith Memorial Basket-
  ball Hall of Fame,
  145–148, 208
Nantucket, MA, 112
Nantucket Whaling Mu-
  seum, 112
Naismith, Dr. James, 145–
  148
Nathan Hale Homestead,
  42
Nature centers
  Audubon Center (Green-
    wich, CT), 208
  Stamford Museum and,
    209
Naumkeag, 142
Nautilus Memorial Subma-
  rine Force Library and
  Museum, 187–190
New Bedford, MA, 112
New Bedford Whaling Mu-
  seum, 112
New England Air Museum,
  209
New England Carousel
  Museum, 167–170,
  208

New England industries,
  75–113
New England Maple Mu-
  seum, 85, 86, 88
New England Ski Museum,
  152–154
New England Sports Mu-
  seum, 155–158, 208
New England sugar
  houses, 85–88
New Hampshire Farm Mu-
  seum, 112
Newport, RI, 23–27, 72,
  124–127, 142, 149–151,
  208
Newport, VT, 113
Newport Casino, 149–151
Norlands Living History
  Center, 108–111, 208
Norman Rockwell Exhibi-
  tion, 200
The Norman Rockwell Mu-
  seum at the Old Cor-
  ner House, 197–199
Norman Rockwell Museum
  in Rutland, 200
North Adams, MA, 96,
  208
North Andover, MA, 112
North Bennington, VT, 142
North Fairfield, VT, 57,
  58–60
Northhampton, MA, 72
Norwalk, CT, 138–141, 208

Old House (Adams'), 46–
  47, 48
Old New-Gate Prison and
  Copper Mine, 34–37
Old North Church (Bos-
  ton), 41
Old South Meeting House
  (Boston), 41
Old State House (Boston),
  41
Old State House (Hart-
  ford), 42
Old Sturbridge Village,
  194–196
Old Wethersfield, CT, 20–
  22
Old York Historical Society
  museums, 16–19
Olde Towne Doll Shop, Old
  Wethersfield, 22
Owls Head Transportation
  Museum, 173, 174

Park-McCullough House,
  142
Parks
  Acadia National, 201–204
  at Battleship Cove, 95–
    96
  Boston National Histori-
    cal, 41, 208
  Fort Griswold, 42
  Gardner Heritage, 96
  Holyoke Heritage, 96
  Lawrence Heritage, 95
  Lowell Heritage, 95
  Lowell National Histori-
    cal, 80–82, 84, 208
  Lynn Heritage, 95
  Minutemen National His-
    torical, 42
  Putnam Memorial, 42
  Western Gateway Heri-
    tage, 93
Patten, ME, 112
Paul Revere's House, 41
Pawtucket, RI, 80, 82–84
Peabody Museum, 209
Peary-MacMillan Arctic
  Museum, 209
Penobscot Marine Museum,
  112
Pierce, Franklin, 49–52
Pierce Homestead, 49–52
Pierce Manse, 51–52
Pilgrim Hall Museum, 13,
  15, 208
Pittsfield, MA, 112
Planetarium, Fairbanks
  Museum and, 209
Plant, Thomas Gustave,
  133–134
Plimoth Plantation, 11–12,
  14–15
Plymouth, MA, 1116, 208
Plymouth Notch, VT, 56–
  58
Plymouth Rock, 13–14
Poland Springs, ME, 112
Portland, ME, 128–131,
  209
Portland Museum of Art,
  209
Portsmouth, NH, 31–33,
  42, 142
Portsmouth, RI, 176
Portsmouth Trail, 42
Presidential homes and ar-
  tifacts, 43–74
Proctor, VT, 113, 135–137

Providence, RI, 142
Putnam Brothers Sugar House, 88
Putnam Memorial State Park, 42
Putney, VT, 87

Quincy, MA, 45–48

Red Barn Christmas Shop (Old Wethersfield), 22
Redding, CT, 42
Revere, Paul, House, 41
Richard Sparrow House, 14, 15
Rock of Ages Granite Quarry, 105–107
Rockland, ME, 173, 174
Rockwell, Norman, 197–200
Roosevelt, Franklin D., 6164
Roosevelt Home, 61–64
Rosecliff, 142
Rutland, VT, 200

Salem, MA, 42, 209
Sandwich, MA, 176
Saugus, MA, 77–79
Saugus Iron Works National Historic Site, 77–79
Science Museum of Connecticut, 209
Searsport, ME, 112
Seashore Tolley Museum, 173–175
Shaker Museum, 112
Shaker Village Canterbury, 89–92 Hancock, 112
Shelburne, VT, 159–162
Shelburne Museum, 159–162
Ships Mayflower II, 12–13 USS Constitution, 38, 41, 183
Shopping, Old Wethersfield, 22
Simsbury, CT, 421–627 House, 14–15
Ski Museum, New England, 152–154
Slater Memorial Museum

and Converse Art Gallery, 208
Slater Mill, 82–84
Slater Mill Historic Site, 80, 84
Smith's Castle, 42
"The Sporting Lady of Bellevue Avenue," 149–151
Sparrow House, 14
Sports Museum, New England, 155–158, 208
Sports museums, 143–158
Springfield, MA, 145–148, 208
St. Johnsbury, VT, 113, 209
St. Johnsbury Athenaeum, 209
Stamford, CT, 209
Stamford Museum and Nature Center, 209
Sterling and Francine Clark Art Institute, 209
Stockbridge, MA, 42, 142, 197–199
Strawbery Banke, 31–33
Stuart and John's Sugar House, 88
Sturbridge, MA, 194–19
Sugar houses, 85–88
Sweet Gatherings (Old Wethersfield), 22
Synagogue, Touro, 24–25, 27

Taft, William Howard, 72–73
Tennis Hall of Fame, 149–151, 208
Thomas Bailey Aldrich House, 32
Touro Synagogue National Historic Site, 24–25, 27
Toys in the Attic (Old Wethersfield), 22
Transportation museums, 171–175
Tuck Memorial Museum, 176

USS Constitution, 38, 41, 183
USS Nautilus, 187–190

Vermont Marble Exhibit, 113
Victoria Mansion, 128–131
Volleyball Hall of Fame, 176

Wanton-Lyman-Hazard House, 26, 27
Webb-Deane-Stevens Museum, 21, 22, 208
Wells, ME, 175
Wells Auto Museum, 175
Wenham, MA, 176
Wenham Historical Association and Museum, 176
Wentworth-Coolidge Mansion, 142
West Harford, CT, 68–71, 208, 209
Westerly, RI, 176
Western Gateway Heritage State Park, 93–95, 96, 208
Westmoreland, NH, 88
Wethersfield, CT, 208
Weymouth, MA, 72
Wheelwright House, 33
"Whites of Their Eyes," 41, 208
Wickford, RI, 42
Williamstown, MA, 209
Wilson, Colonel Herbert L., 135–137
Wilson, Woodrow, 73
Wilson Castle, 135–137
Wilson Museum, 42
Windsor, CT, 42
Windsor, VT, 113
Windsor Locks, CT, 209
Winter sights, 177–209
Wiscasset, ME, 176
Wistariahurst, 142
Woodstock, VT, 101–104, 176
Woodstock Historical Society's Dana House, 176
Worcester, MA, 179–182

Yesteryears Doll and Miniature Museum, 176
York Village, ME, 16–19

Other Books from The Countryman Press, Inc.

Explorer's Guides

Explorer's Guides focus on independently owned inns, motels, and restaurants, and on family and cultural activities reflecting the character and unique qualities of the area.

The Hudson Valley and Catskill Mountains: An Explorer's Guide, by Joanne Michaels
and Mary-Margaret Barile, $15.00
Maine: An Explorer's Guide, Sixth Edition,
by Christina Tree and Mimi Steadman, $17.00
New Hampshire: An Explorer's Guide,
by Christina Tree and Peter E. Randall, $17.00
Vermont: An Explorer's Guide, Fifth Edition,
by Christina Tree and Peter S. Jennison, $16.95

Books About New England

Canoeing Massachusetts, Rhode Island and Connecticut
Revised Edition, by Ken Weber, $10.00
Family Resorts of the Northeast,
by Nancy Pappas Metcalf, $12.95
Fifty Hikes in the White Mountains, Fourth Edition,
by Daniel Doan, $12.95
Maine Memories, by Elizabeth Coatsworth, $10.95
Mount Washington, by Peter E. Randall, $9.95
The New England Herb Gardener,
by Patricia Turcotte, $14.95
25 Bicycle Tours in Vermont, Second Edition,
by John Freidin, $10.00
Walks & Rambles in Rhode Island, Second Edition,
by Ken Weber, $11.00

These books are just a sample of the variety of fiction, nonfiction, and outdoor recreation guides we offer. Our books are available in bookstores and specialty stores, or may be ordered directly from the publisher. Shipping and handling costs are $2.50 for 1-2 books, $3 for 3-6 books, and $3.50 for 7 or more books. To order, or for a catalog, please write to The Countryman Press, Inc., Dept. APC, P.O. Box 175, Woodstock, Vermont 05091. Prices and availability are subject to change.